From Stress to Stress

From Stress to Stress

An Autobiography of English Prosody

Burton Raffel

Archon Books 1992

First published 1992 as an Archon Book, an imprint of
The Shoe String Press, Inc., Hamden, Connecticut 06514

Printed in the United States of America

The paper used in this publication meets the minimum requirements of
American National Standard for Information Sciences—Permanence of Paper
for Printed Library Materials. ANSI Z29.48-1984 ⊛

Library of Congress Cataloging-in-Publication Data

Raffel, Burton.
From stress to stress ; an autobiography of
English prosody / Burton Raffel.
p.   cm.
Includes bibliographical references.
1. English language—Versification.
I. Title
PE 1505.R28   1992   92-10538   821.009—dc20
ISBN 0-208-02330-5 (alk. paper)

The poet and his readers may not be able to formulate explicitly the nature of the [metrical] constraints that are operative in a given poem; there is little doubt, however, that neither the poet nor the experienced reader would find great difficulty in distinguishing wildly unmetrical lines from lines that are straightforwardly metrical. . . . We shall look upon these readily observable abilities of experienced poetry readers as crucial facts that must be accounted for by an adequate theory of prosody. Such a theory, however, should be expected to do more than this; it should also help us to illuminate the relationship between a speaker's everyday linguistic competence and his ability to judge verses as metrical or unmetrical and as complex or simple.

We propose that the aforementioned ability of readers and poets to make judgments about verse lines is due to their knowledge of certain principles of verse construction. This knowledge, much like the average speaker's knowledge of his language, is in general tacit rather than explicit. When questioned, people may be unable to give a coherent statement of the principles that they employ in judging verse lines in terms of metricality and complexity. It is therefore the task of the metrist to provide a coherent and explicit account of this knowledge, just as it is the task of the grammarian to make explicit what is known by the fluent speaker of a language.

Morris Halle and Samuel Jay Keyser
English Stress: Its Form,
Its Growth, and Its Role in Verse
(N.Y., Harper, 1971), pp.139–40

to the two hundred graduate students, more or less,
who over the years studied
(and sometimes fought about)
prosody with me

Contents

Introduction

As its subtitle indicates, this is not a theoretical book. But it does have a controlling theory, and that theory inevitably determines a great deal about the documentation which forms the bulk of the book. Most of that documentation is drawn from the primary historical record, which of course means from the surviving corpus of English-language poetry, 800–1990 A.D. That is, what the poets in fact *do* is what the prosody of poetry written in English in fact *is*: understanding what the poems tell us is not only the crucial but in a sense the only task. But since there is also a sometimes fascinating, though much less complete and not always completely clear secondary historical record, consisting of pamphlets, essays, and correspondence about prosodic matters, I have included selections from this material as well, especially from its most uproarious period, the latter part of the sixteenth century. Finally, a small quantity of modern linguistic explanation and commentary is also included, notably in the early portions of the book, since not many literary critics and metricists seem fully aware of its powerfully elucidative significance. I have not however included material from what might be called the tertiary record, namely, twentieth-century scholarship about prosody. A very full, though in its annotative comments not always reliable, guide to that scholarship is T.V.F. Brogan, *English Versification, 1570–1980: A Reference Guide* . . . (Baltimore, Johns Hopkins University Press, 1981). Like many metricists, Brogan sees prosodic questions far too abstractly: unlike after-the-fact theoreticians, poets necessarily deal with prosody concretely and almost exclusively in hands-on fashion. The difference in approach makes for an enormously different kind of understanding, and it is primarily the poets' understanding, embodied in and readily decipherable from their practice, which seems to me important. To understand what metricists have argued, over the years, is an interesting byway of cultural history. But it has remarkably little to do with the actual history either of poetry or of prosody. Actual history is my sole concern.

Some of the items here reprinted are prefaced or followed by my own commentary, usually brief. Like the primary and secondary material, this commentary necessarily draws on the book's controlling theory. It seems therefore only fair to at least sketch out that theory, in a kind of barebones outline. It has been framed exclusively on the basis of primary material exactly like (but of course much larger in scope than) that printed in the pages which follow. I can only ask that anyone to whom the theory seems either strange or erroneous try to suspend judgment. Metricists can legitimately argue with one another. I do not think they have a right to argue with historical fact.

The surviving corpus of Old English (also known as Anglo-Saxon) poetry is the oldest in any modern European tongue. I prefer to employ the rubric "Old English," because except under extraordinary circumstances, and over immense periods of time, languages do not change their fundamental characteristics. English at any period is English—clearly different in detail as between, say, the language of *Beowulf* and that of *The Waste Land*, but just as clearly English, for all that. Languages certainly evolve; they just as certainly change, and they also die. But even under the onslaught of cataclysmic political and cultural events, a language that manages to survive, like the people who speak it, usually remains in most of its basic characteristics pretty much the same language. Lexicon is most immediately subject to pressure, and thus to change, but though it may appear the most basic of all linguistic characteristics, lexicon—or vocabulary—is in truth much less fundamental than such larger phenomena as morphology and phonemic (as opposed to purely phonetic) structure. A language is a functioning cultural *system* and, as in any system, it is the overall principles which most shape the system's end result, not the component parts by means of and upon which the system operates. We have many variations on this theme, in the historical record, but nothing which seems to me to contravene the rule. Why this should be so, though it can be learnedly discoursed upon, is here much less important than the simple fact that, like all cultural givens, it is what it is.

English is what linguists call a stress-phonemic language. That is, in English as in German, Russian, and other stress-phonemic tongues, shifts in stress can create shifts in meaning. *CONtent*, in English, is a totally different word—having a different morphological role as well as a different lexical signification—from *conTENT*. By no means all English words shift meaning and function when their stress is changed. *MORphine*, for example, is in usage and meaning identical to *morPHINE*. But the fact that stress-shifts *can* and *do* produce shifts in both meaning and function is part of a whole network of linguistic consequences, some of which will be detailed later in this book. Among other things, to accord stress this sort of importance creates for every native speaker of the language the expectation, whether conscious or not it does not matter, that stress is actively of consequence and must constantly be paid attention to. When we speak, in ordinary conversation, or when we read aloud from an English text of any sort—telephone book, shopping list, calculus handbook—we are careful to employ stress and un-stress, in various degrees and according to principles and patterns most of which we cannot here pause to discuss. Listen to yourself talking on the telephone, or reading aloud from the daily newspaper, and you will hear not only this constant variation in stress, but also a kind of supervening pattern, rough but recurrent and very palpable. The basic nature of this pattern is a sequence of first lesser and then greater stress: English stress *rises*, as it were, and then falls off, only to rise again, on and on ad infinitum. Elaborate studies have confirmed that for all native speakers of English the dominant pattern is exactly this sequence of less stress followed by more stress. (Which means, as later pages will demonstrate, that truly trochaic verse is very nearly impossible in English: most of what has been labelled trochaic has been quite simply misunderstood.) Metricists and others call this sequence an iambic pattern. For prosodic purposes, it is perhaps the single most important fact about the English language; the ramifications of this basic and built-in metrical pattern are almost unending. Nor does it make any difference whether we personally approve or disapprove: like the sun that shines and the rain that falls, the underlying iambic pattern of English *is*. We do not have to like

xiii

sunshine or rain for the one to glow and the other to drop to the ground.

Other languages exhibit other patterns. The largest group of languages employs a syllabic pattern; differences in stress may be noted, to be sure, but they are not in the same sense meaningful. Stress in French may for example convey emphasis, or assorted other subtleties, but this is not as basic a linguistic feature as is the phonemic stress of English, which changes meaning, morphology, and the like. The syllabically organized language family includes the various Romance languages, French, Spanish, and so on, and a good many non-European tongues too. Malay/Indonesian is syllabic—and like all syllabic languages has a syllabic prosody in which stress plays no role. There are tonal languages, most especially Chinese, in which the particular musical sequence (level, level/up, level/down, level/down/up) changes meaning. In Chinese, for example, "Ma-Ma-Ma-Ma," properly pronounced, means "Mother scolds the horse."

This is not a full list of possible or historical linguistic patterns, any more than we can exhaust syntactical possibilities, worldwide, by talking of "verbs" and "nouns" and "adjectives," all of which are categorizations which emerge from our conceptual system and frequently reflect nothing whatever in other languages. Written Chinese being constituted of "characters" rather than "words," the Chinese dictionary is structured according to a character's number of radical stroke marks. The Hebrew dictionary is structured according to *gesher*, or root; the Malay-Indonesian dictionary is organized according to yet another kind of root, upon which the language operates with a unique agglutinative morphology of pre- and post-particles, none of which exist or even correspond to anything in any Indo-European language.

Given its basic stress-organized patterns, it is hardly surprising that throughout its history the English language has employed a prosody in which stress has always played a major role. Old English prosody, to compress hotly disputed complexities into a few elementary but basic principles, combines patterns of recurring alliteration with a usual (though not quite invariable) pattern of four stresses to a poetic line. Confronted with the very different prosody of French, and after the Norman Conquest of 1066 confronted with it most directly and powerfully, English prosody evolved over a period of three or four hundred years what can be called (though Chaucer did not originate it) the Chaucerian Compromise. Destined to become the regnant prosodic principle in English, after about 1540, the Chaucerian Compromise (1) drops the governing role of alliteration, (2) adds a French-derived requirement of a particular syllable count for a particular line, but (3) preserves the fundamental and essentially unalterable native English stress principle. Rhyme is added, too, but no matter how important it may be poetically, rhyme is of no great prosodic significance: it will not be dealt with in this book.

This was a linguistic and artistic solution that literally took centuries to evolve, and still further centuries to securely perpetuate. The records are unfortunately fragmentary, over the years between the Norman Conquest and the triumphant emergence of Geoffrey Chaucer. But what written information we do have (there is of course no other information but writing, for that era) allows us to trace out at least some of the false starts, and to see in general the Chaucerian Compromise's main developmental outline. (Whether or not Celtic prosody had a role is not clear, and will not be dealt with in these pages.) We do not have enough information: that should be clear simply from the existence of the socalled "Alliterative Revival," an astonishing emergence from long years of silence of a much-changed and debased form of Old English prosody, in poems as different and memorable as *Sir Gawain and the Green Knight* and *Piers Plowman*. This phenomenon, as I have elsewhere argued, is better termed the "Alliterative *Sur*vival"; it is surely a re-emergence, a re-surfacing of literary techniques that had for several centuries gone underground, rather than anything new. (It is particularly fascinating to find the "Alliterative Survival" surfacing, to the North, in many of the poems of a leading Scottish Chaucerian, William Dunbar. But neither Dunbar's nor any other "Alliterative Survival" poetry will be dealt with in these pages.) There is surely both a class and a political dimension, here: the new ruling class being French, the stubborn practitioners of English poetry, and especially old-style English poetry, could not have been a favored minority. Lacking any solid historical record, however, we are limited to sheer conjecture—and though conjecture is decidedly tempting, and may quite possibly be accurate, I prefer to abstain.

But the mysterious loss of prosodic certainty among Chaucer's direct poetic descendants, in England proper, from about 1400 to 1540, coupled with the plain fact of continued prosodic competence in Scotland's English-language poets during those same years, indicates a historical complexity still waiting to be understood. I would like nothing better than to explain it; like many others, I have wrestled with the known facts and I cannot make full sense of them. But we do know that, with Surrey and Sidney, the Chaucerian Compromise reasserted itself in England—though not all at once, and certainly not in the clearest of terms. The secondary material in the pages which follow is mostly drawn from the half century of often confused polemics and groping which follow Surrey and Sidney's once-again firmly consistent practice, somehow lost by Chaucer's followers, Lydgate and Hoccleve, and even by Surrey's older contemporary, Sir Thomas Wyatt. By about 1600, the confusion is gone—at least in practice, which is what matters—and we move into what might be called the Golden Age of the Chaucerian Compromise. It is the poets of the later Elizabethan and the Jacobean eras who pretty much define the "classical" procedures of English prosody.

The details must be left for the pages which follow. It must however be remembered that what we are dealing with *is* a compromise. "Classical" English prosody is a practical way of harmonizing two different prosodic traditions; it is also simply one aspect of a general fusion of two different languages and ways of life, primarily founded in English speech and ways but heavily influenced as well by French. By the latter part of the thirteenth century, the once natively-French conquerors began to need books to help them learn French; native English roots were blossoming again, and native literary flowers were beginning to show through. By the fifteenth century one could use English instead of French in some of the law courts, and in the royal court, too. Chaucer's friend John Gower, who had begun his poetic career writing in French, later switched to the culturally (politically?) safer Latin—and at the end of his career shifted again, revealingly, to English. English, whether spoken or written, remained as I have said English, and it is clear from the historical record that over the centuries, and particularly from the late thirteenth century on, French slowly died out in England as a natively spoken tongue, leaving to be sure a huge residue of French-derived words in the English lexicon (and French-derived customs elsewhere in the native culture).

We have no aural transcriptions; we do not know exactly how Chaucer, or Hoccleve, or Surrey, sounded when they read their poems aloud, though we know they did so read them. And as with all compromises, we need to be alert to the differently aimed and constituted vectors of which the final product is necessarily composed. In particular, we need to be alert to the two standards by which all poetry in literate cultures is always read: (1) the formal prosodic standard, and (2) what can be termed the spoken (or "linguistic") standard. That is, although in an oral culture there is only one basic standard (though there may be and invariably are internal variations thereon, both over time and as between different reciters), in a literate culture poetry exists as it were both in men's eyes (on the page) and in their ears (when read aloud), and there are inevitably differences in the way poetry is sounded when read, solitary and usually silently, to oneself, and when it is read aloud in a company of others. Further: when a literate culture has evolved, as English did, a compromise prosodic convention, incorporating features from two deeply different poetic cultures, there cannot help but be a necessary degree of tension as between the spoken (linguistic) standard, framed as it must be only in terms of the native English tradition, and the formal prosodic standard, framed as it is partly in terms of the native English but also in terms of the foreign French tradition.

This tension, as the pages which follow will demonstrate, is a powerful and, after roughly half a millenium of practical application and slow evolution, still a dispositive factor. Again, the details must await the evidence. But a few of the basic highlights of the formal Chaucerian Compromise, as it was over time fitted together and put into practice, should be preliminarily noted:

1. Stress is always metrically governing, but this is relative rather than normal spoken (linguistic) stress. That is, since it is defined by a kind of poetically supervening cultural agreement (convention), prosodic stress is not necessarily identical to, though ideally it should not stray too far from, spoken (linguistic) stress. (There has been an attempt to call prosodic stress "accent," reserving "stress" for more purely linguistic contexts. I believe this double usage more confusing than clarifying; it also seems to me to weaken metrical understanding by appearing to disconnect prosodic from linguistic stress.)

2. Prosodic stress being something which is specified by prosodic rules and agreements—that is, by convention—rather than by normal linguistic procedures, it is a kind of stress which can

be defined only within the particular prosodic measure, which for English poetry after the Chaucerian Compromise means the poetic foot (a prosodic concept completely unknown to Old English times).

3. Formal scansion is thus a foot-by-foot affair; prosodic values do not carry over from one foot to another, regardless of other normal linguistic factors like syntax. Punctuation is thus no more reliable a guide to prosodic scansion than is grammar, though in the classical period, and in the work of the better poets, both punctuation and grammar are usually made to work with rather than against prosodic convention.

What subsequently happens to this classical prosodic standard, as the evidence will show (though no more evenly and neatly than anything else in human history), is in no way surprising to anyone acquainted with linguistic and macro-cultural analysis. By the eighteenth century, there is (see in particular the work of Alexander Pope) a kind of anticipatory re-tightening of the prosodic screws—the kind of prelude-to-the-storm that a twentieth-century linguist, had there been one on the scene, might well have seen for what it truly was. What this anticipatory re-tightening meant, in a word, was that the hard-won linguistic compromise was threatening to slowly unravel. Native linguistic forces had gradually, over time, asserted themselves more and more strongly against alien, foreign importations. The eighteenth-century reaction was in that sense a quasi-desperate holding action, doomed to failure.

And fail it did. The poetry of that quintessential outsider, William Blake, is a clear warning of the coming prosodic storm, though precisely because he was an outsider he was not taken seriously—was not indeed thought entirely sane. (We tend to forget how insignificant was Blake's poetic reputation, until long after his death.) But deep signs of prosodic trouble can be seen even in the outwardly unexceptionable work of poets like Shelley and Keats, prosodic cracks and fissures which deepen as the nineteenth century proceeds, finally ending in the violent irregularities of Browning and Swinburne, and the outright rebellion of Gerard Manley Hopkins, which all but discards the remnants of the once-glorious Chaucerian Compromise.

Not so much an outsider as, in part, a foreigner of a different kind (i.e., an American), Walt Whitman pushed even more heavily against a prosodic tradition hundreds of years old and not so much dying as, again, piece by piece unravelling. Much of twentieth-century English prosody, still a source of sorrow to many, has seen what can be thought of as the sad triumph of vers libre. "Mere anarchy," we hear from all sides, has been "loosed upon the world." But from the longer and larger perspective here outlined, this emergence of what amounts to a new kind of stress-based prosody must be seen as simply the re-emergence of what could not forever be suppressed, namely, the native power and nature of the English language, still stress-phonemic after all these years. Classical Chaucerian Compromise prosody, half a millenium old, is not dead; it neither need nor will die in the foreseeable future. But venerable as it is, it has been obliged to share the poetic platform with, just as in the future it will be obliged to make accommodations to, a set of linguistic and prosodic facts more than twice as old still. *Beowulf* has not been re-born in our time, nor has Modern English turned back to Old. But "the child is father to the man," and Old English remains, willy-nilly, in our bones, and our mouths, and our ears.

I am not so foolish as to assert about my theory (neither did Keats: he carefully put the words into the mouth of his ancient urn) "that is all/ Ye know on earth, and all ye need to know." The history of English prosody is not ready to be written out in full, and certainly not by me. But old poems, like old stones, do speak, and this book is the record of what they, not I, have to tell us. Prosody is hardly the beginning and ending of poetics; metricists have a natural tendency to over-emphasize what prosody accomplishes and what its study can explain. But prosody is an important part of poetics and of poetic history; for whatever that may be worth, prosody is crucially important to poets; and to understand how it works, and used to work, and to some extent why, is surely one significant key to the poems which remain at the center of proper literary study. We are not John Donne, nor were we meant to be. But it is better to know than not to know how John Donne probably meant us to read, and to scan, and in a way thus to appreciate and even to understand, his poems.

This book's prosodic notation

In the interests of the reader, the printer, and the publisher (that is, to heighten readability, reduce typographical complexity, and lower printing costs), no special markings are here used to indicate prosodic scansion. Indeed, since metrical stress and unstress are strictly bipolar—within a given foot, a syllable is either stressed or unstressed—only two scansion markings are used in this book. In all the poetic passages here reproduced for scansion purposes:

1. a syllable printed in capital letters is a syllable scanned as having metrical stress; a syllable printed in lower-case letters is thus a syllable not having metrical stress. To put it the other way around, any syllable not printed in capital letters is not metrically stressed.

2. poetic feet are separated by slashes (/).

Thus:

> i THINK/ that I/ shall NE/ver SEE/
> a PO/em LOVE/ly AS/ a TREE/ . . .

3. in non-indented quotes, lineation is noted by two slashes (//).

4. Lines, or portions thereof, of indeterminate scansion are in lower case letters and italicized.

1 / The General
Dominance of Language

a. Verse, whatever else it is, is a manipulation of linguistic givens.

(W.K. Wimsatt, "Foreword," *Versification: Major Language Types*, N.Y. U. Press, 1972, p.xi)

b. The nature of language is of vital concern to those who study literature, because language is the medium in which literature is written, just as the chemistry of paint and the science of optics are important for historians of art. It is a mistake to think that the "creative artist," whether in literature, painting, sculpture, music or any other field, is wholly free and untrammeled by "material" considerations. Every artist's work is conditioned by the limitations of the medium within which he works . . . Hence the literature written in any given language is of course channeled, insofar as its possibilities of expression are concerned, by the structure of the language. This latter determines what can and cannot be said in the language, and limits the means at the literary artist's disposal . . . This influence is exerted at every level of linguistic structure, from the phonological through the syntactic, and of course in lexicon as well.

(Robert A. Hall, Jr., *Introductory Linguistics*, Philadelphia, Chilton, 1964, p.406)

c. The complexities of metre, as they appear to us, are really complexities of varied rhythmical patterns in ordinary spoken language. . . . As a rule, the rhythms of language are allowed to suggest the regularities of metre. Once the regularities have been

1

promoted, however, the composer feels them as a binding law, the reader as a pattern of expectations.

(Walter Nash, *Our Experience of Language*, N.Y., St. Martin's, 1971, pp.158–59)

d. An economy—not an abundance—of linguistic features generates metrical patterns.

(Harvey Gross, *Sound and Form in Modern Poetry*, Ann Arbor, U. of Michigan Press, 1964, p.31)

2 / The Particular Dominance of The English Language

a. Ours is an accentual or stress language. . . . We are habituated to stress; we depend on it, and are disappointed almost viscerally when it is sparse. None of this would hold true, however, for a language in which stress is weaker than in English (for example, . . . modern French and classical Greek).

As we read a line of verse, we are unconsciously so eager, as it were, to get to a primary stress, that we tend to race past the weaker syllables.

(Karl Shapiro and Robert Beum, *A Prosody Handbook*, N.Y., Harper, 1965, pp.17, 22)

b. Because English is a much more accentual language than, for example, the Romance tongues, stress has generally played a more significant part in the structure of English verse than it has in many continental poetries.

The English language appears most naturally to organize its rhythms in ascending patterns; that is, the main instinct in English poetry is for iambic or occasionally anapestic movements, rather than for trochaic or dactylic.

(Paul Fussell, *Poetic Meter and Poetic Form*, rev. ed., N.Y., Random House, 1979, p.62)

c. The most important single factor in the historical development of English and its present-day structure is stress. . . . The importance of stress in English, however, runs far deeper than its impact on either spelling or pronunciation. For stress—by means of its phonemic, morphological, syntactical, rhetorical, rhythmi-

3

cal, and semantic modifications—is the key determinant of most of the major attributes of Modern English: simple inflectional system and fixed word order, poor correspondence between spelling and pronunciation, word-group cadences, and the enormous flexibility of functional shifts due to the placing of accents.

. . . Stress further determines the suprasegmental (intonation) features of English: *pitch* (levels of intonation), *juncture* (pause values), *prolongation* (quantitative emphasis), and *pacing* (speed of speech delivery). . . . And stress is the key to juncture, pitch, and the intonational contours of Old English.

(John Nist, *A Structural History of English*, N.Y., St. Martin's, 1966, pp.5–6, 116)

d. The way in which the utterance of syllables is timed, i.e., the *rhythm* of their utterance, differs from one language to another, and there are at least two distinct types of timing. In one type (as found in Italian, French, Spanish, etc.) the rate of utterance of a succession of syllables remains approximately the same no matter how many stresses there are or where they fall in the stream of speech; an utterance of, say, ten syllables will take approximately twice as long as one of five syllables. This type of rhythm is known as *syllable-timed*, since it is determined by the number of syllables (stressed or unstressed). In another type of rhythm (such as we have in English), the stressed syllables in an utterance come at evenly spaced intervals, and any unstressed syllables falling in between the stressed ones are simply fitted in with greater or lesser speeding up as may be necessary. In this type of rhythm, which is known as *stress-timed*, a breath-group containing, say, two stressed syllables will take up the same amount of time no matter whether there are no, one, or five unstressed syllables in between.

. . . Since English and the other Germanic languages are stress-timed, the meter of our verses is determined by the number of recurrent stresses in the line. . . . In the Romance languages, which are not stress-timed, but syllable-timed, a system of versification depending on recurrent stresses is not possible . . . Ever since late medieval times, when French lost phonemically significant stress entirely, the use of a regular number of syllables and of rhyme has been the only characteristic distinguishing French verse from prose.

(Hall, *Linguistics*, pp.64, 406–07)

4

e. The trouble with syllabic verse—as that verse is called in which the length is determined by the number of syllables—is that [in English] the ear does not hear the units. No one hearing or reading this poem says intuitively, "Ah, a fifteen syllable line!: It takes some detective work to discover the pattern—and when one has it, what has he?

(Judson Jerome, *Poetry: Premeditated Art*, Boston, Houghton Mifflin, 1968, p.99)

f. The structure of a Greek sentence, with its dependent clauses and intricate welding of parts into a whole, cannot be reproduced in English, which lacks the syntax to do it. Even devices so common and so natural as compound adjectives seldom look at home in English and tend to hinder the flow of a sentence. Where Greek binds together, English must break up. . . . Since Greek meter is built not, like ours, on an uncertain and shifting scheme of accent but on a fixed and easily grasped scheme of quantity, in which what counts is not the stress put on a word but the time which it takes to pronounce it and the assumption that all syllables are either long or short and that a long syllable is the equivalent of two shorts, Greek is capable of effects quite beyond the capacity of English. Nothing can be done about this, and nobody has succeeded in the smallest degree in turning Greek choral meters into English.

(Maurice Bowra, "Foreword," in Bacchylides, *Complete Poems*, trans. Robert Fagles, New Haven, Yale U.P., 1961, pp.xii-xiii)

g. Stress patterns are basic to clear communication in English, and are often difficult for the non-native speaker to master. They provide a logical and distinguishing feature for abstracting and formalizing poetic measure appropriate to English.

(Susanne Woods, *Natural Emphasis: English Versification from Chaucer to Dryden*, San Marino, Huntington Library, 1984, p.5)

h. It would be quite untrue to say that there is always an equal interval between stresses in English. It is just that English has a number of processes that act together to maintain the rhythm. . . . It is as if there were a conspiracy in English to maintain a regular rhythm. However, this conspiracy is not strong enough to completely override the irregularities caused by variations in the number and type of unstressed syllables.

(Peter Ladefoged, *A Course in Phonetics*, N.Y., Harcourt Brace Jovanovich, 1982, pp.109–110)

5

3 / Old English
(Anglo-Saxon) Prosody

a. The typical Anglo-Saxon line of verse was divided by a caesura [pause] into two approximately equal half lines, with
strongly stressed syllables in each. . . . The first initial sound of
the second half-line gave the alliteration for the entire line, and it
was repeated in at least one other stressed syllable, as in "a
gristly ghost, Grendel by name." The numbers of unstressed
syllables separating stressed ones were not regularly fixed as in
modern English.

> (Margaret Schlauch, *English Medieval Literature* . . . , London,
> Oxford U. Press, 1967, pp.13–14)

b. The Old English alliterative verse lines had a specified number
of vowels with primary stress but . . . required, in addition, that
the consonant clusters preceding certain stressed vowels in the
line alliterate.

> (Halle and Keyser, *English Stress*, p.147)

c. Stress and time being nowhere *necessarily* correlative, syllable
length (physiological, etymological, positional, or whatever) may
be discounted in [old English] rhythmic analysis. Unlike classical
Latin meters, Old English poetry determines stress by alliteration, natural accent, rhetorical emphasis, and syntactical priority
(in that order).

> (Neil D. Isaacs, *Structural Principles in Old English Poetry*, Knox-
> ville, U. of Tennessee Press, 1968, p.168)

d. "Caedmon's Hymn," West Saxon version, orthographically
adjusted to indicate pronunciation: late 7th century

6

NUW shulon HERiyan HEOfonriches WARD,
MEOtudes MAHta and his MODyaTHANC,
WORC WULdorfaeder, swa hey WUNdra yeHWAES,
ECHa DRIHten, OR onSTALda.
hey AERest SCOP EORthan BARnum   5
HEOfon tow HROfa,   HALiy SHIPpend;
tha MIDdanYARD   MONcunnes WARD,
ECHa DRIHten,   AEFter TEYoda
FIRum FOLdan,   FREY aelMIHtig.

4 / The 12th Through the
14th Centuries (Pre-Chaucer)

a. MYRie SUNGen the MUNeches* BINnen eLY†
    tha CNUT KYNG REW ther BY:
    "ROWeth, KNItes, NOER the LAND
    and HERe WE thes MUNeches SAENG."
    (ca. 1150)

*probably not pronounced trisyllabically
†a famous monastery
tha = when
knites = knights

This is clearly not Old English stress-prosody, but no exact
scansion is possible. The fourth line is arguably iambic tetrameter. If "here" (hear) is monosyllabic, the line could however
have been intended to scan: "and HERE WE thes MUNeches
SAENG." It is even possible, in such a time of unsettled prosody,
that (again, with "here" monosyllablic) the line could have been
scanned with only three metrical stresses, "and HERE we thes
MUNeches SAENG." It is safest to say only that the fourth line
looks rather like iambic tetrameter: what was (and wasn't) in the
poet's mind and ears is at best uncertain. "Most Middle English
lyric verse is based on stress-rhythm rather than on syllable-
rhythm. Even when successive lines of a poem regularly show,
say, eight syllables alternating by degree of stress, it is the stress
that establishes the rhythm." (Robert D. Stevick, "Introduction," *One Hundred Middle English Lyrics*, ed. Robert D. Stevick, Indianapolis, Bobbs-Merrill, 1964, p.xxvii)
    The three consecutive stresses of the second line fit no English

8

pattern except perhaps the Old English one, though three consecutive stresses without intervening unstressed syllables is a disputable reading in Old English scansion. The third line *appears* to be largely what we would call trochaic. The first line is to some extent problematic, more than likely scanned as here indicated, but—since the rest of the poem probably has four stresses per line—line one just possibly may also contain only four stresses, either with "binnen" unstressed, perhaps even elided (i.e., treated as if monosyllabic, since the following word begins with a vowel), or else with both syllables of "myrie" unstressed. We can reduce line one to four stresses, however, only if we presuppose some controlling pattern, more or less on the model of Old English scansion. And any such assumption seems at best dubious.

Therefore, there being no clear pattern—that is, no clear sense of what the poet was thinking and he and his audience were hearing—it is impossible usefully to mark foot divisions (if any were contemplated: I suspect none were, though this "poem" may well have been part of a longer dance-song, perhaps even its refrain).

b.   MIRie it IS, while SUMer iLAST,
         with FUGheles SONG.
         oc NU NECHeth WINdes BLAST,
         and WEDer STRONG.
         ey! EY! WHAT, this NIGHT is LONG!   5
         and ICH, WITH well MICHel WRONG,
         SORegh and MUrne* and FAST.
               (ca.1225)

   ─────────────────
   *probably elided
   oc = but
   necheth = comes on, begins

Roughly seventy years later, prosodic confusion still reigns. Scanned strictly in terms of stress per line, the "pattern" here makes a kind of sense: 4–2–4–2–4–4–3. But not only is this pattern very differently constituted from one in, say, a superficially similar seventeenth-century prosodic sequencing, it is also somewhat illusory. The later metrical convention, for example, which allows a pair of monosyllabic words with equivalent linguistic stress (as in line 5, "Ey! Ey!") to be scanned so that the second alone takes a *metrical* stress, seems unlikely to have existed in the early thirteenth century. I am uncertain about the scansion of line one. It could be argued that it makes better prosodic sense scanned completely differently, with five rather than four metrical stresses: "MIRie IT is, WHILe SUmer iLAST." (The unstressed first syllable in "ilast" could also be elided, so that the word contains only a single metrical syllable.) This might be more or less trochaic, though the short second and fourth lines are basically iambic, as is English itself. But the proper scansion of line three is unknowable. Why not: "OC nu NECHeth WINdes BLAST"? Without prolonging this brief discussion, it is fair to say that the metrical uncertainty in lines five through eight, too, is marked. There are many alternative readings that could sensibly be argued for.

In short, since all prosodic patterning must be both conventional (i.e., agreed upon) and consistent, the *in*consistencies in this early thirteenth century poem indicate fairly plainly that there is still no prosodic pattern. Which is another way of saying that Middle English did not quite yet have what we can call a prosody.

c.   SUM/er IS/ iCU/men IN/ —
        LHU/de SING!/ cucCU./
        GROW/eth SED/ and BLOW/eth MED/
        and SPRINGTH/ the WU/de NU —/
        SING!/ cucCU./   5
            SING!/ cucCU,/ nu. SING!/ cucCU./
            SING!/ cucCU./ SING!/ cucCU nu./
        AW/e BLE/teth AF/ter LOMB,/
        LHOU/th* AF/ter CAL/ve CU./
        BUL/luc STER/teth, BUC/ke VERteth,/   10
        MU/rie SING!/ cucCU./
        cucCU,/ cucCU,/
        wel SING/es THU,/ cucCU —/
        ne SWIK/ thu NA/ver NU!/
            [repeat refrain]   15
                (ca. 1250? 1280? 1310?)

----
*lhouth = bisyllabic
sterteth = jumps
verteth = farts
swik = cease

10

Whatever its exact date—controversy reigns—this little dance-poem, for which we are fortunate enough to have musical notation, clearly crosses from metrical uncertainty to something very like the Chaucerian Compromise. Accordingly, I here begin the practice of marking off likely foot divisions. Lines seven and sixteen (the second line of the refrain) are a little uncertain, however, nor is the musical notation sufficiently precise to help us scan the final word. Taking my cue from line ten, which unmistakeably uses a feminine ending, I have somewhat tentatively scanned lines seven and sixteen with a total of four feet and, like line ten, with a feminine ending. The consistent alternation of four and three feet throughout the poem also argues against giving lines seven and sixteen an extra foot. There is of course the theoretical possibility of not one but two alternative scansions: (1) putting a metrical stress on the final "nu" in lines seven and sixteen, thus making that word a separate metrical foot, or (2) reading the entire line not as iambic but trochaic. I reject both these abstractly conceivable possibilities, but wish here to deal only with the second, the first being of much less importance. (That is, the scansion of the poem as a whole would not be much different even were the final "nu" in the refrain to be separately stressed.)

English as a language is as I have noted natively iambic in its tendencies: lines four, twelve, thirteen, and fourteen are plainly so scanned. Though I doubt that the poet was thinking in such terms, or that he was consciously aware of the "beheaded iamb" (that is, letting a stressed syllable start a line but immediately reverting to iambic meter: this was to become perhaps the most common metrical "irregularity" in all of traditional English prosodic usage), the poem is so conclusively English that, despite fierce temptation to argue for an original written in some other tongue, scholars have always been essentially unanimous that this was a text written in English in the first place. And not only is the swing of the melody, as well as the swing of the verses, powerfully iambic, but the single most important word, "cuccu," is consistently and repeatedly employed so that an iambic measure is the only one into which it can be fitted. The refrain, for example, *cannot* be scanned to a trochaic measure: "SING! cuc/ CU nu/" is an impossibility. Spring and its avian harbinger, the rising call of the cuckoo, would be sadly betrayed by any attempt to force an abstract trochaic meter onto so concretely iambic a bird song. This being a dance, it is readily apparent why no less than twelve of the poem's sixteen lines would begin, appropriately, with a foot-stamping thump. But no dancer, and no musician, would accept the argument that an emphatic initial beat is intended to set the entire metrical pattern for what follows. An emphatic initial beat, in a word, is meant simply and solely to get things in motion, to start dance and music and singing with a literal bang.

In the years that followed the composition of this poem (whatever its exact date), thousands of English poems composed according to the Chaucerian Compromise metric were to contain innumerable lines that begin with a stress. Most of those later poems would also share the emphatic assertion of an iambic movement (again, a consistent *rising* metric that matches the rising movement of English itself). There have sometimes been metrically naive readers, even metrically naive scholars who, seeing rather than hearing their scansions, have been deceived by this usage of what came to be called the beheaded iamb. But metrical analysis is neither for the naive nor, as every good poet knows, for those with visual rather than aural biases (or for those with tin ears).

d.   BRYNG/ us IN/ no BROW/ne BRED/ fore
         THAT/ is MAD/ of BRAne;/
    nor BRYNG/ us IN/ no WHYT/bred,* fore
         THER/in IS/ no GAme,/
    but BRYNG/ us IN/ good ALe./

    BRYNG/ us IN/ no BE/fe for THER/ is MA/ny BOnys;/
    but BRYNG/ us IN/ good AL/e, for THAT/ goth
         DOWNE†/ at ONys./   5
    and BRYNG/ us IN/ good ALe./ . . .
                  (early 14th cent.: excerpt)

---

*see discussion, below
†elided

The last three stanzas of this eight-stanza wassail song feature second lines of seven rather than six feet, in the underlying 4–3 pattern so common in traditional English prosody: "nor BRYNG/

us IN/ no PYG/ges FLESCH,/ for THAT/ wyl MAK/ us BORys";
"nor BRYNG/ us IN/ no VEN/iSON/, for THAT/ is NOT/ for owr
GOOD"; "nor BRYNG/ us IN/ no DOK/es FLESCH,/ for THEI/
SLOBer/ in the MER." It may therefore be that other lines are
also to be given seven rather than six feet, as follows: "BRYNG/
us IN/ no WHIT/ BRED"; "BRYNG/ us IN/ no BE/FE . . . ,"
and so on. Fluctuations of this sort are inherently likely when a
new prosodic synthesis is being forged.

e.   i HAUE*/ a NEW/e GARdyn,/
                    and NEW/e IS/ beGUNne;/
                    SWYCH/ an OTH/er GARdyn/
                    know I/ not UN/der SUNne./

                    in the MID/dis OF/ my GARdyn/   5
                    IS/ a PER/yr SET,/
                    and it WEL/e NON/ per BERN/
                    BUT/ a PER/ ienET./ . . .
                    (early 14th cent.: excerpt)

*elided
peryr = pear
bern = bear
ienet = early

Irregularities obviously continue. Note how "peryr" in line six is
spelled "per" in line eight, clearly for metrical reasons. Line four
could as likely be scanned: "KNOW i/ not UN/der SUNne/":
there is no particular metrical consistency about the fourth line
of any of the poem's six stanzas (which also argues for an
uncertainty about replicative form). The fourth stanza, for example, ends: "che DED/e in FILle,/" meaning "she gave me (in
quantity) to partake of." This can be given three metrical feet
only if it is scanned (as it may well have been): "CHE/ DEDe/ in
FYLle./" Since only the last stanza has a final line that does not
begin with a stress ("but NON/ per I/onET/"), the stress on
"che" may well be called for.

f.   lo! LEM/man SWE/te, now MAY/ thou SE/
                    that I/ haue LOST/ my LYF/ for THE./
                    what MYGHT/ i DO/ the MAre?/
                    forTHI/ i PRAY/ the SPE/ciaLI/

that THOU/ forSAKE*/ ill COM/paNY/   5
that WOUN/des ME/ so SAre./ . . .
(ca. 1375: excerpt)

---

*elided
lemman = sweetheart, darling
mare = more
sare = sore

5 / *Chaucer*

a. . . . GLORi/ous MAYDE*/and MOO/der, WHICH/
    that NEvere/
   were BIT/ter, NEITH/er in ER/the NOR/ in SEE,/
   but FUL/ of SWEET/nesse* AND/ of MER/ci EVere,/
   HELP that/ my FA/der BE/ not WROTH/ with ME./
   speak THOU,/ for I/ ne DAR/ not HIM/ ySEE,/   5
   so HAVE*/ i DOON/ in ERTHE*,/ alLAS/ the WHIle!/
   that CER/tes, BUT/ if THOU/ my SO/cour BEE,/
   to STINK/ eTERNE/ he WO/le my GOST/ exILe./ . . .
           (Geoffrey Chaucer, "An ABC," ca. 1369: excerpt)

---

*elided
but if = unless
gost = spirit

   Geoffrey Chaucer is thought to have been born about 1340,
perhaps as late as 1343 or 1344. Although there is uncertainty
about the chronology both of Chaucer's life and his work, by
about 1375 he had definitely composed *The Book of the Duchess*
and a good deal of shorter poetry. Again, Chaucer did not
originate what I have called the Chaucerian Compromise. But it
was his example that solidified, expanded, and in almost all ways
ensured the future of what we now call traditional English prosody, and in particular the dominance of the iambic pentameter
line. Although he experimented with a variety of line-lengths (*The
Book of the Duchess*, almost thirteen hundred lines long, is in
iambic tetrameter), Chaucer's special contribution was the regu-
larization and popularization of iambic pentameter. His early

usage, as seen here, is fluent and assured—neither so regular as to be mechanical, nor so irregular as at any point to break the pattern. Something just under fifty percent of the poem's twenty-three stanzas begin with what I will hereafter term a "reverse iambic foot": none employ the previously noted beheaded iamb. As we will see throughout this book, the first foot of a stanza is of all metrical positions the most likely to exhibit one or the other sort of irregularity, so that either a beheaded iamb or a reverse iamb in that position cannot really be thought of as anything but more or less regularly (conventionally) irregular. Note that it is the sense of the line—the opposition of "thou" and "I"—rather than any sort of convention about two syllables of essentially equal stress which leads me to stress "thou" rather than "spek," in line five. This illustrates a working principle of considerable importance: prosodic conventions generally operate *only* when there is no evidence to controvert or supplant them. That is, evidence is evidence; it is concrete and decisive. But conventions are abstract and usually operate only by default.

b.   the DOU/ble SOR/we of TRO/iLUS/ to TELlen,/
       that WAS/ the KYNG/ priAM/us SONE*/ of TROYe,/
       in LO/vynge,† HOW/ his AV/enTU/res FElen/
       fro WO/ to WELE*,/ and AF/ter OUT/ of JOIe,/
       my PUR/pos IS,/ er THAT/ i PAR/te FRO ye./   5
       theSI/phoNE,/ thow HELP/ me FOR/ (t')‡ enDIte/
       thise§ WO/ful VERS,/ that WE/pen AS/ i WRIte./
       (Chaucer, *Troilus and Criseyde*, ca.1386: Book I, stanza 1)

---

*elided
†final "e" probably not pronounced
‡the prosodic (as opposed to the grammatical)
apostrophe convention: see below
§probably bisyllabic, but (in part because of the
unstressed syllable which ends line six) at least
arguably monosyllabic.

Our *grammatical* apostrophe convention, in which the apostrophe substitutes for a deleted vowel (as in "it's," "doesn't"), is rather like the orthographical convention in French, whereby a *circonflexe* accent replaces a deleted "s" (as in *hôtel*, *côte*). But what we see in Chaucer's sixth line, here, is something quite different, namely, the *prosodic apostrophe* convention. It signals that poet and reader agree to *scan* (*not* to read) "t'enDITE" as bi- rather than trisyllabic. The licence is a modest and relatively inconspicuous one, and convenient for a sometimes hard-pressed poet.

No apostrophe can make up for a syntactic omission: words needed to make good grammatical sense cannot be conjured out of linguistic existence, nor can a poet's metrical urgencies change the requirements of the English language. John Dryden argues, in the 1697 preface to his translation of the *Aeneid*, that in fact a poet should only invoke the prosodic apostrophe when it makes linguistic sense—that is, when current linguistic usage might well omit a metrically undesirable syllable. But Dryden also cheerfully admits that "I have not strictly observed [this rule] myself," nor is there any doubt that other poets too disregarded it. Here is a flagrant example from Ben Jonson. The first prosodic apostrophe, here, is unexceptionable, since in Jonson's time "livest" could be either mono- or bisyllabic. But consider the second:

COB, thou/ nor SOUL/dier, THIEFE,/ nor FEN/cer ART,/
yet BY/ thy WEA/pon LIV'ST!/ th'hast ONE/ good PART./
("To Pertinax Cob," Epigram LXIX)

Again, Chaucer's (as well as many other poets') use of the prosodic apostrophe is closer to linguistic standards than is Jonson's. I cannot help adding, finally, though it obliges me to deal still further with matters as yet two hundred years in the future, that in order to make his awkward verses seem perfectly metrical, Jonson is perfectly capable of using the prosodic apostrophe as a signal that the reader must regard an entire word, consonant(s), vowel and all, as metrically nonexistent:

then HIS/ chast WIFE, though BEAST/ now KNOW/
no MORE,/
he'adUL/ters STILL:/ his THOUGHTS/ LYE with/
a WHORE./
(Jonson, "On the Same Beast," Epigram XXVI)

There will be a good deal more to say about Jonson's metrical practice, and in particular about its contrast with that of John Donne, later in this book.

17

c. biFIL/ that IN/ that SE/son ON/ a DAY,/
   in SOUTH/werk AT/ the TA/bard AS/ i LAY/
   REdy/ to WEN/den ON/ my PIL/griMAge/
   to CAUN/terBU/ry* with FUL/ deVOUT/ coRAge,/
   at NYGHT/ was COME†/ inTO‡/ that HOS/telRYe/   5
   wel NYNE†/ and TWEN/ty IN/ a COM/paigNYe,/
   of SON/dry FOLK,/ by A/venTURE†/ yFALle/
   in FE/laweSHIPE†, and PIL/grimes* WERE*/ they ALle,/
   that TO/ward CAUN/terBUR/y WOL/den RYde./
   the CHAM/bres AND/ the STA/bles WE/ren WYde,/   10
   and WEL/ we WE/ren ES/ed AT/te BESte./
   and SHORT/ly, WHAN/ the SON/ne WAS/ to RESte,/
   so HADDE†/ i SPO/ken WITH/ hem EVE/riCHON/
   that I/ was OF/ hir FE/lawe/SHIP/ anON,/
   and MA/de FOR/ward ER/ly FOR/ to RYse,/   15
   to TAKE†/ oure* WEY/ ther AS/ i YOW/ deVYse./
                         (Chaucer, "General Prologue,"
                         Canterbury Tales, ca. 1387: excerpt)

---

*vowel reduced?
†elided
‡shifting stress, in Chaucer's time

18

6. / *England Immediately after Chaucer*

a.   of HEM/ that WRI/ten OUS/ toFOre/
     the BO/kes DUELLE*/, and WE/ therFOre/
     ben TAWHT/ of THAT/ was WRI/te THO:/
     FORthi/ GOOD is/ that WE/ alSO/
     in OU/re TYME*/ aMOUNG/ ous HIEre/   5
     do WRYTE*/ of NE/we SOM/ maTIEre,/
     esSAMP/led OF/ these* OL/de WYse/
     so THAT/ it MYHTE*/ in SUCH/ a WYse,/
     whan WE/ ben DEDE*/ and EL/esWHEre,/
     beLE/ve TO/ the WORL/des EEre/   10
     in TY/me CO/mende* AF/ter THIS./ . . .
          (John Gower, "Prologus," *Confessio Amantis,*
                                    ca. 1386: excerpt)

     _____

     *elided
     duelle = remain
     tho = then
     beleve = be left

b.   GO, li/tle PAM/fiLET,/ and STREIGHT/ thee DRESse/
     unTO/ the NOB/le ROOT/id GEN/tilESse/
     OF/ the MYGH/ty PRINCE*/ of FA/mous hoNOUR,/
     my GRA/cious LORD/ of YORK,/ to WHOSE†/
        noBLESse/
     me RE/coMAN/de *with hertes humblesse,*/   5
     as HE/ that HAVE†/ his GRACE*/ and HIS/ faVOUR/
     FOWNden/ alWAY;/ for WHICH/ i AM/ detTOUR/

                          19

for HIM/ to PREYE*;/ and SO/ shall MY/ symPLESse/
HERti/ly DO/ unTO/ my DE/thes HOUR./
(Thomas Hoccleve, "Balade to My
Gracious Lord of York," early 15th cent.: excerpt)

---

*elided
†monosyllabic?

The spellings "humbly" and "humbely" both occur in Chaucer's
work; the former is presumably bi- and the latter tri-syllabic.
Accordingly, if "humblesse" in line five, above, has four rather
than the spelling-indicated three syllables, the latter part of the
line can be scanned: "with HER/tes HUM/b(e)lESse./" If this is
not the case, then the line cannot be scanned as iambic pentameter or indeed as any other recognizable meter.

c. AEFter/ that HER/vest IN/ed HAD/ his SHEves,/
and THAT/ the BROU/ne SEA/son of MY/helMESse/
was COME*/, and GAN/ *the trees robbe of ther leves,/*
that GRE/ne had BENE*/ *and in lusty fresshnesse,*
hadd DY/en *and doune throwne undar foote,*   5
that CHAUN/ge SANK/ inTO/ myne HER/te
ROOte./ . . .
(Thomas Hoccleve, "The Complaint,"
early 15th cent.: excerpt)

---

*elided

The only way that line three can be scanned as iambic pentameter
is: "the TRE/es ROBBE*/ of ther LEVes./" "Trees" as a bisyllabic word is dubious but more or less possible in Hoccleve's
time—that is, a licence but arguably a defensible one.

But I can see no possible way of scanning either line four or
line five as iambic pentameter. In this poem, as in Hoccleve's
work generally, there is an excess of unstressed syllables—itself
a sign of metrical insecurity. But the unscannable lines are even
plainer evidence. Nor do they occur simply now and then: in the
next stanza of "The Complaint" we find this line: "That sta-
blenes in this world is there none." This has ten syllables, to be
sure. But how can it be scanned as iambic pentameter, the
apparent governing metric of the poem? In the same stanza we

20

also find this line: "Endure it shall not; he shall it forgon." Again, it is hard to scan this as iambic pentameter, nor is any sign, in this or in other stanzas, that Hoccleve has deliberately varied his metric, whether to fit some formal variation or for any other recognizable reason. The first line of the third stanza can just barely be scanned as iambic pentameter, though exceedingly bad iambic pentameter: "which FOR/ to WEYVE*/ is IN/ no mAN/ nes MYGHT." Line three, however, staggers even more markedly, though one can scan it more or less appropriately: "and IN/ the ENDE*/ of noVEM/bar upON/ a NYGHT./" But by the time we come to the second line of the fourth stanza, it is clear that Hoccleve, for whatever reason, simply has no firm handle on iambic pentameter: "[Since I] Was scourged, clowdy hath bene the favoure . . ."

How the key to Chaucerian Compromise meter was so quickly lost in England (but, as we shall see in a moment, retained in Scotland), remains unknown. Hoccleve, of course, is not the only loose-jointed bard on display:

d.   *Problemys of olde likenesse and figures,*
     Whiche proved been fructuous of sentence,
     and hath/ aucTOR/ite GROWN/ded IN/ scripTURes,/
     by RE/semBLAUNCES/* of NO/billr* AP/paRENce/,
     Withe moralites concluding of prudence,   5
     like AS/ the BI/bylle reHER/sithe BY/ wriTING./
     how TREES/ someTY/me CHASE*/ himSELF/ a
           KYNG./

                    (John Lydgate, "The Churl and the Bird,"
                                           ca. 1410?: excerpt)

---

*monosyllabic?

The first line perhaps be squeezed into the iambic pentameter mold: "PROBlemys/ of OLD/e LI/kenesse AND/ figURes,/" in part by eliding "problemys" into only two syllables and "likenesse" into only three (perhaps even two?). The result is defensible, though not remarkably attractive. Similarly, line two might arguably be scanned: "whiche PRO/ved BEEN/ frucTU/ous OF/ senTENce,/" though this too leaves something to be desired. Even the fifth line can be bent into some degree of

21

metrical compliance: "with MO/raLITES/ conCLU/ding OF/ pruDENce/"—but the torturing of "moralites" hardly seems either a realistic possibility or, indeed, worth the trouble. A more likely, but metrically impermissible scansion, would be: "WITH/ moRAL/iTES/ conCLU/ding OF/ pruDENce,/" which in its turn can be made metrically permissible, if not exactly metrically brilliant, by scanning: "with morAL/iTES/ conCLU/ding OF/ pruDENce./" If "moralites" is thus read as a plainly French-derived word, however, with something like an *accent aigu* on the "e," it would seem that "auctorite" in the third line should almost certainly be read the same way. But this produces metrical havoc—or, at least, a kind of hexameter line in the midst of a pentameter pattern. Even the "proper" lines do not show much metrical firmness. It is not quite sufficient to say that Lydgate sometimes employs a "cryptic style, abounding in headless lines, trochaic rhythms, and epigrammatic jerkiness" (John Lydgate, *Poems*, ed. John Norton-Smith, Oxford University Press, 1966, p.xi), just as it begs the point to explain of Hoccleve's work that "the verse is as a rule mechanical, unmusical" (*Chief British Poets of the Fourteenth and Fifteenth Centuries*, ed. W.A. Neilson and K.G.T. Webster, Houghton Mifflin, 1916, p.430).

e.   whan i reMEM/bre aGAYN/
    how mi PHI/lyp was SLAYN,/
    never HALFE/ the PAYNE/
    was beTWENE/ you TWAYNE,/
    PYramus/ and THESbe,/
    as THAN/ beFELL/ to ME:/
    i WEPT/ and i WAYLED,/

    the TEA/rys downe HAYLED;/
    but NO/thynge it aVAYLED/
    to call PHY/lyp aGAYNE,/

whan I/ reMEM/bre aGAYN/
HOW/ my PHI/lyp was SLAYN,/
NE/ver HALFE/ the PAYNE/
WAS/ beTWENE/ you TWAYNE,/
PY/raMUS/ and THESbe/   5
as THAN/ beFELL/ to ME:/
i WEPT/ AND/ i WAYLED,/

the TEA/rys DOW/ne HAYLED;/
but NO/thynge IT/ aVAYLED/
to CALL/ PHYlyp/ aGAYNE,/

22

whom GYB/ our CAT/ hath   /whom GYB/ our CAT/
   SLAYNE.   hath SLAYNE./
(John Skelton, "Phyllyp Spa-
   rowe," c.1505: excerpt)

One of Skelton's recent editors observes that the so-called "Skel-tonic" is "distinguished by 2–3 accents per line. The stresses are often underscored by alliteration, which, in turn, may link to-gether two or three lines." (Philip Kinsman, "Introduction," John Skelton, *Poems*, Oxford University Press, 1969, p.xviii) Another way of saying this, of course, is that Skelton (a) has no particular grip on the Chaucerian Compromise and (b) works fairly clearly in the shadow of the primal Old English metric. I have set out two quite different scansions of this passage, but other variations are also possible. In line one, for example, the first foot may well be scanned "WHAN i," and the first foot of line two similarly reversed, "how MI." Again, it is the plain fact of metrical uncertainty which needs to be underscored. There is no way of recovering precisely what Skelton thought he was up to, metrically, for from early Skeltonics to late, there is no clear standard established.

f.   o THOUGHT/ful HER/te, TOM/bled ALL/ aBOUte/
        upON/ the SE/ of STOR/my IG/noRAUNce,/
        For to sayle forthe thou arte in grete doute,
        Over/ the WAVES*/ of GRE/te EN/comBRAUNce;/
        Wythout ony comforte, saufe of esperaunce,   5
        whiche THE/ exHOR/teth HAR/deLY/ to SAYLE/
        unTO/ thy PURpose/ wyth DI/liGENT/ traVAYLE./
                  (Stephen Hawes, "The Pastime of
                     Pleasure," 1506: excerpt)

---

*elided

Line seven is metrically defective; line four is appropriately scannable only if "waves" is rather dubiously elided and "Grete" is equally dubiously not. Lines three and five seem beyond help. Hawes was English, indeed Oxford-educated.

7 / *Scotland after Chaucer*

a.   ane DOO/lie SES/soun TO/ ane CAIR/full DYTE/
    suld COR/resPOND/ and BE/ eQUI/vaLENT:/
    richt SA/ it WES/ quhen I/ beGAN/ to WRYTE/
    this TRA/geDIE —/ the WED/der RICHT/ ferVENT,/
    quhen A/riES,/ in MID/dis OF/ the LENT,/   5
    SCHOris/ of HAILL/ can FRA/ the NORTH/
        disCEND,/
    that SCANT/lie FRA/ the CAULD/ i MICHT/
        deFEND./

                    (Robert Henryson, "The Testament of
                    Cresseid," ca.1480?: excerpt)

---

doolie = sad
cairfull = sad
dyte = poem
fervent = hot
defend = protect

b.   quhen PAILL/ auRO/ra with FA/ce LA/menTAbill/
    hir RUS/sat MAN/till, BOR/derit ALL/ with SAbill,/
    LAPpit/ aBOUT/ the HE/vin*ly CIR/cumSTANce,/
    the TEN/der BED/ and AR/res HO/norAbill/
    of FLO/ra, QUE/ne till FLOU/res A/miAbill,/   5
    in MAY/ i RAIS/ to DO/ my OB/serVANce,/
    and EN/terit IN/ a GAR/dyne† OF/ pleSANce,/

with SOL/ dePAINT/ as PA/raDICE†/ aMIA*bill‡,/
and BLIS/ful BE/wis with BLO/med VA/ryANce./
(Gavin Douglas, "The Palice of Honour," undatable:
Douglas was born about 1475 and died in 1522; this poem
was first published in 1553: excerpt)

*elided?
†elided
‡shifting stress
rais = hurry
depaint = brightly painted
bewis = boughs
blomed = flower-covered

c. at MA/tyne* HOURE*/ in MI/dis OF/ the NICHT,/
WALKnit/ of SLEIP/ i SAW/ beSYD/ me SOne/
ane* AI/git MAN/ semit SEX/tie YEIRIS*/ of SICHT/
this SEN/tence† SETT/ and SONG/ it IN/ gud TOne:/
"omNI/poTENT/ and E/terne GOD/ in TROne,/
to BE/ conTENT/ and LUFE†/ the I/ haif CAUS/
that my LICHT/ yowTHE/id IS/ oPPREST/ and DOne;/
HOnour/ with A/ge to EV/ery† VER/tew DRAwis. . . ."/
Walter Kennedy, "Honour With Age": undatable: Kennedy
was born about 1460 and died in 1508: excerpt)

*elided
†elided?
sone = at once ("soon")
of sicht = appearance
yowtheid = youth

8 / Wyatt, Surrey, and Sidney

a. they FLE/ from ME/ that SOME*/tyme* DID/ me SEke/
   with NA/ked FO/te STAL/king IN/ my CHAMbre./
   i HA/ve SENE*/ them GEN/till TAME†/ and MEke/
   that NOWE†/ *are wyld and do not remembre*
   that SO/meTY/me* they PUT/ theimSELF/ in
   DAUNger/   5
   to TA/ke BRED/ at my HAND;/ and NO/we they RAUNge/
   BEsel/ly SE/king WITH/ a conTIN/uel CHAUNge./
      (Sir Thomas Wyatt, "They Flee From Me," fl.1530–40,
                  Muir, *Wyatt*, Poem 37: excerpt)

---

*elided?
†elided

The discrepancy between the scansion of "sometyme" in lines
one and line five is probably impermissible; it is however the only
way that line one can be preserved as iambic pentameter. If
"sometyme" is scanned in both lines as it is scanned in line five,
line one would scan like this: "they FLE/ from ME/ that SO/me
TY/me DID/ me SEke/," which is of course hexameter and not
permissible. On the other hand, if "sometyme" is scanned in line
five as I have scanned it in line one, then line five would be left
with no firm metrical pattern at all.

More: line four can be more or less bent into iambic pentameter, if we scan "wyld" as bisyllabic—not at all an impossibility
in Wyatt's day, though certainly not the most likely scansion.
Line four would thus read: "that NOWE/ are WY/ld AND/ do

NOT/ reMEMbre.'' This is at best a shaky possibility—and given the other roughnesses in this first stanza of Wyatt's best-known lyric, I have preferred to leave line four metrically resolved. Lines one and five are problematic, as I have said. There is no certainty that "fote" in line two would still have been bisyllabic for Wyatt, though it might well have been. But if "fote" was in fact monosyllabic, line two is metrically unsatisfactory. Line six probably contains thirteen syllables, which is high for iambic pentameter of an acceptable smoothness—and indeed the line is not at all smooth. Neither is line seven. "There seems to be no particular reason," writes Kenneth Muir in his edition of Wyatt, "why Wyatt . . . should lose the secret of the iambic pentameter." But as Muir adds, of Wyatt's roughly 120 lyrics "the worst of them [are] crabbed and ineffective, a few in the halting verse of his immediate predecessors and contemporaries." (*Collected Poems of Sir Thomas Wyatt*, ed. Kenneth Muir, London, Routledge and Kegan Paul, 1949, pp.xix, xxiii) D.W. Harding, though convinced that "we can at least put aside the older idea that Wyatt was groping and fumbling towards a regularity of metre that lack of skill prevented him from achieving," is still obliged to concede that, at times, "the rhythm [scansion] is . . . defeating, and it must be admitted that puzzles remain about Wyatt's intention." (D.W. Harding, "The Poetry of Wyatt," in *The Age of Chaucer*, ed. Boris Ford, Harmondsworth, Penguin, 1965, p.205)

Those puzzles are notoriously greater in the pioneering translations Wyatt made from the Italian, introducing the sonnet form into our language, and in the sonnets he wrote directly in English.

b.   how OFT/ have* I,/ my DERE*/ and CRU/ell FOO,/
           with THOSE/ your IYES/ for TO/ get PEACE*/
           and TRUYse,/
        profferd you myn hert, but you do not use
           eMONG/ so high THINGES†/ to CAST/ your
           MYNDE†/ so LOWE†./
        if any othre loke for it, as ye trowe,   5
           there VAYN/ weke† HOPE†/ doeth† GREATE/ly
           THEM/ abUSE;/
        and thus I disdain that that ye refuse;
           it WAS/ ons MYN:/ it CAN/ no MORE†/ be SO./

yf I/ then it CHASE†,/ nor IT/ in YOU/ can
        FYNDE‡/
    in THIS/ exILE†/ no MAN/ner OF/ comFORT,/   10
    nor LYVE*/ alLONE†, *nor where he is called*
        resort,
He/ may WAN/der FROM/ his NA/turall† KYND./
    so SHALL/ it BE/ great HURT/ unTO/ us
        TWAYN,/
    and YOURS/ the LOSSE*/ and MYN/ the DED/ly
        PAIN./

                                (Muir, *Wyatt*, Poem 32)

*elided
†elided?
‡the rhyme with "kynd"
strongly suggests elision

The scansion of the first two feet of line four seems at best
doubtful, and certainly metrically unsatisfactory. So too line
nine. The beheaded iamb which may begin line twelve hardly
seems metrically appropriate, especially since the last syllable of
line eleven, immediately preceding, is almost certainly stressed
(whatever the scansion of line eleven may be). Indeed, the concluding couplet seems almost as different from the body of the
poem, metrically, as does the bob and wheel in *Sir Gawain and
the Green Knight* from the loosely alliterative stress metric of the
bulk of that poem.

c. *who so list to hount, I knowe where is an hynde,*
        but AS/ for ME,/ heLAS,/ i MAY/ no MORE*:/
        the VAYNE*/ traVAIL/ hath WE/ried ME/ so
            SORE*./
    i AME†/ of THEIM/ that FAR/thest COM/meth
        beHINDE*;/
    yet MAY/ i BY/ no MEANES*/ my WE/ried MYNDE*/   5
        drawe* FROM/ the DIERE*:/ but AS/ she
            FLEETH*/ aFORE*,/
    FAYNting/ i FO/lowe*. I/ leve OF[F]/ thereFORE*,/
        SINS in/ a NETT/ i SEKE*/ to HOLD/ the
            WYNDE*./

                        28

who LIST/ her HOUNT,/ i PUT/ him OWTE†/ of
    DOWBTE*,/
as WELL/ as I/ may SPEND/ his TYME†/ in
    VAIN:/   10
and, GRA/ven with DI/amONDS,/ in
    LET/ters PLAIN/
there is written her faier neck rounde abowte:
NO/li ME/ tanGER/e, for CE/sars i AME*;/
and WYL/de FOR/ to HOLD,/ though I/ seme*
    TAME*./

                                 (Muir, *Wyatt*, Poem 7)

---

*monosyllabic?
†elided
list = wishes, desires

d. w. RES/teth HERE,/ that QUICK/ could NE/ver REST;/
whose HEA/venly GIFTES*/ enCREA/sed BY/
    disDAYN/
and VER/tue SANK/ the DE/per IN/ his BREST:/
such PRO/fit HE/ by EN/vy COULD/ obTAIN./
a HED,/ where WIS/dom MIS/teRIES/ did FRAME;/   5
whose HAM/mers BET/ STYLL in/ that LIVE/ly
    BRAYN/
as ON/ a STITHE,/ where THAT/ some WORK/ of
    FAME/
was DAY/ly WROUGHT/ to TURNE/ to BRI/taines
    GAYN./

a VI/sage STERN/ and MYLD;/ where BOTHE/ did
    GROW/
VICE to/ conTEMNE,/ in VER/tue TO/ reJOYCE;/   10
aMID/ great STORMES/ whom GRACE/ asSUR/ed SO/
to LYVE/ upRIGHT/ and SMILE/ at FOR/tunes
    CHOYCE./

a HAND/ that TAUGHT/ what MIGHT/ be SAYD/ in
    RHYME;/
that REFT/ CHAUcer/ the GLO/ry OF/ his WIT;/

a MARK/ the WHICH,/ unPAR/fiTED/ for TIME,/
some MAY/ apPROACH,/ but NE/ver NONE/ shall
HIT./ . . .

                (Henry Howard, Earl of Surrey,
            "Wyatt resteth Here," 1542: excerpt)

---

quick = alive
stithe = anvil
unparfited = not perfected?

Wyatt's name, the first word in the poem, is abbreviated, to (a) confine the word to one syllable and thus (b) keep it metrically unstressed, so that the pentameter metric can be preserved. This usage plainly parallels the prosodic apostrophe, though unlike the latter it is a rarity, even in the unsettled conditions of mid-sixteenth-century poetics, and seems never to have attained any significant foothold. Surrey's meter—which as one of his editors, Emrys Jones, nicely observes, is the true core of his slender but permanent historical importance (Surrey, *Poems*, ed. Emrys Jones, Oxford University Press, 1964, p.xxiii)—is smooth but not at all slavishly so. Lines six, ten, and fourteen feature inverted feet. (The first foot of line sixteen may also be intended to be metrically inverted: the evidence is insufficient for an absolutely clear decision either way.) As the scansion of this poem also shows, Elizabethan English was by Surrey's time manifestly losing the vocalized final "e." Only "encreased," in line two, demands the extra syllable so common in Middle English. We could say that the immediately following vowel, in line ten, makes it necessary to elide "contemne," as the immediately following vowels in line twelve make it necessary to elide "lyve" and "smile"; we could even argue that it is the vowel of "encreased" in line two which keeps "giftes" monosyllabic. But though some final "e" syllables might conceivably have been pronounced, here, like the rhyme-words "fame," "rejoyce," and "time," it seems plain from "turne" in line eight, "visage" and "bothe" in line nine, as well as "vice" in line ten that the language was phasing out the final "e" as anything but an orthographic vestige. See too the next poem, also by Surrey.

e.　when WINDE/sor WALLES/ suSTAINED/my
　　　　WEA/ried ARME,/
　　my HAND/ my CHYN,/ to EASE/ my REST/less
　　　　HEDD,/
　　each PLEA/sant PLOT/ reVEST/ed GREEN/ with
　　　　WARM,/
　　the BLOS/somed BOWES/ with LUS/tie VEARE/
　　　　ySPRED,/
　　the FLOW/red MEADES,/ the WED/dyd BIRDS/
　　　　so LATE/　　　　　　　　　　　　　　　　　　5
　　myne EYES/ disCOV/ered. than DID/ to MYND/
　　　　reSORT/
　　the JOI/ly WOES,/ the HATE/less SHORTE/ deBATE,/
　　the RAK/hell LIFE/ that LONGES/ to LOVES/
　　　　disPORTE./
　　wherWITH,/ alAS,/ myne HE/vy CHARGE/ of CARE/
　　HEAPT in/ my BREST/ brake FORTH/ aGAINST/ my
　　　　WILL,/　　　　　　　　　　　　　　　　　　10
　　and SMO/ky SIGHES/ that O/ver CAST/ the AYER./
　　my VA/pored EYES/ such DRE/ry TEARES/ disTILL/
　　　　the TEN/der SPRING/ to QUIC/ken WHER/ thei
　　　　FALL,/
　　and I/ half BENT/ to THROWE/ me DOWN/ withALL./
　　　　　　　　　　(Surrey, "When Windesor Walles," 1537?)

revested = clothed, attired
veare = spring
hateles = friendly

f.　LOving/ in TRUTH,/ and FAINE/ in VERSE/ my
　　　　LOVE/ to SHOW,/
　　that SHE/ (deare SHE)/ might TAKE/ some PLEA/sure
　　　　OF/ my PAINE:/
　　PLEAsure/ might CAUSE/ her READE,/ REAding/
　　　　might MAKE/ her KNOW,/
　　KNOWledge/ might PI/tie WINNE,/ and PI/tie GRACE/
　　　　obTAINE;/

> i SOUGHT/ fit WORDS/ to PAINT/ the BLACK/est FACE/
>   of WOE,/   5
> STUDYing*/ inVEN/tions FINE,/ her WITS/ to
>   EN/terTAINE:/
> oft TURN/ing OTH/ers' LEAVES,/ to SEE/ if THENCE/
>   would FLOW/
> some FRESH/ and FRUIT/full SHOWERS†/ upON/
>   my SUNNE-/burn'd BRAINE./
>
> but WORDS/ came HALT/ing FORTH,/ WANTing/
>   inVEN/tion's STAY,/
> inVEN/tion, NA/ture's CHILD,/ fled STEP-/dame
>   STU/die's BLOWES,/   10
> and OTH/ers' FEETE/ still SEEM'D/ but
>   STRAN/gers IN/ my WAY./
>
> thus, GREAT/ with CHILD/ to SPEAKE,/ and
>   HELP/lesse IN/ my THROWES,/
> BITing/ my TREW/and PEN,/ BEATing/
>   mySELFE/ for SPITE —/
> "FOOLE," saide/ my MUSE/ to ME, "LOOKE in/
>   thy HEART/ and WRITE."/
>   (Sir Philip Sidney, "Astrophil and Stella," poem 1, 1582)

---

*bisyllabic?
†monosyllabic?
trewand = truant

This *is* classical English prosody. As the documents in the next section will show, despite the theoretical confusions, terminological uncertainties, and futile quarrels between classically- and vernacularly-minded writers, Sidney's fully achieved practice is thereafter a saving model, a beacon and shining guide, no less for Edmund Spenser than for lesser poets. Sidney's choice of iambic hexameter for the first poem in his sonnet cycle well illustrates his experimental turn of mind. But his deft, fluent handling of the iambic line, though no more "correct" than Surrey's, represents the full recovery of prosodic suppleness, beauty, and power—and his contemporaries and near-contemporaries knew it far more clearly than we seem to.

9 / Elizabethan Prose Documents

a. And in your verses remembre to place euery worde in his natural *Emphasis* or sound, that is to say, in such wise, and with such length or shortnesses, eleuation or depression of sillables, as it is commonly pronounced or used. To expresse the same we haue three manner of accents, *grauis, leuis, et circumflexa,* the whiche I would english thus, the long accent, the short accent, and that whiche is indifferent: the grauve accent is marked by this caracte \, the light accent is noted thus /, and the circumflexe or indifferent is thus signified ~: the graue accent is drawen out or eleuate, and maketh that sillable long whereupon it is placed; the light accent is depressed or snatched up, and maketh that sillable short upon the which it lighteth; the circumflexe accent is indifferent, sometimes short, sometimes long, sometimes depressed and sometimes eleuate. For example of th'emphasis or natural sound of words, this word *Treasure* hath the graue accent upon the first sillable; whereas if it shoulde be written in this sorte *treaSURE,* nowe were the second sillable long, and that were cleane contrarie to the common use wherwith it is pronounced. For furder explanation hereof, note you that commonly now a dayes in English rimes (for I dare not cal them English verses) we use none other order but a foote of two sillables, whereof the first is depressed or made short, and the second is eleuate or made long; and that sound or scanning continueth throughout the verse. We haue used in times past other kindes of Meeters, as for example this following:

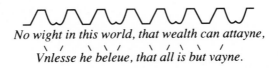

No wight in this world, that wealth can attayne,
Vnlesse he beleue, that all is but vayne.

Also our father *Chaucer* hath used the same libertie in feete and measures that the Latinists do use: and who so euer do peruse and well consider his workes, he shall finde that although his lines are not alwayes of one selfe same number of Syllables, yet, beyng redde by one that hath understanding, the longest verse, and that which hath most Syllables in it, will fall (to the eare) correspondent unto that which hath fewest sillables in it: and like wise that whiche hath in it fewest syllables shalbe founde yet to consist of woordes that haue suche naturall sounde, as may seeme equall in length to a verse which hath many moe sillables of lighter accentes. And surely I can lament that wee are fallen into suche a playne and simple manner of wryting, that there is none other foote used but one; whereby our Poemes may iustly be called Rithmes, and cannot by any right challenge the name of a Verse. But, since it is so, let us take the forde as we finde it, and lette me set downe unto you suche rules or precepts that euen in this playne foote of two syllables you wreste no woorde from his natural and usual sounde. I do not meane hereby that you may use none other wordes but of twoo sillables, for therein you may use discretion according to occasion of matter, but my meaning is, that all the wordes in your verse be so placed as the first sillable may sound short or be depressed, the second long or eleuate, the third shorte, the fourth long, the fifth shorte, etc. For example of my meaning in this point marke these two verses:

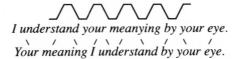

I understand your meanying by your eye.
Your meaning I understand by your eye.

In these two verses there seemeth no difference at all, since the one hath the very selfe same woordes that the other hath, and yet the latter verse is neyther true nor pleasant, and the first verse may passe the musters. The fault of the latter verse is that this worde *understand* is therein so placed as the graue accent falleth upon *der*, and thereby maketh *der* in this worde *understand* to be eleuated; which is contrarie to the naturall or usual pronunciation, for we say *underSTAND*, and not *unDERstand*.

(George Gascoigne, *Certayne Notes of Instruction Concerning the Making of Verse or Rhyme in English*, 1575: excerpt)

b. I like your late English Hexameters so exceedingly well that I also enure my Penne sometime in that kind: whyche I fynd indeede, as I haue heard you so often defende in worde, neither so harde, nor so harshe, that it will easily and fairely yeelde it selfe to our Moother tongue. For the onely or cheifest hardnesse, whych seemeth, is in the Accente; whyche sometime gapeth, and, as it were, yawneth ilfauouredly, comming shorte of that it should, and sometime exceeding the measure of the Number, as in Carpenter the middle sillable, being used shorte in speache, when it shall be read long in Verse, seemeth like a lame Gosling that draweth one legge after hir: and Heauen, beeing used shorte as one sillable, when it is in Verse stretched out with a *Diastole* [i.e., in Latin and Greek poetry, the lengthening of a syllable naturally short], is like a lame Dogge that holdes up one legge. But it is to be wonne with Custome, and rough words must be subdued with Use. For why, a Gods name, may not we, or else the Greekes, haue the kingdome of oure owne Language, and measure our Accentes by the sounde, reseruing the Quantitie to the Verse? . . .

I would hartily wish you would either send me the Rules and Precepts of Arte, which you obserue in Quantities, or else followe mine, that M. Philip Sidney gaue me, being the very same which M. Drant deuised, but enlarged with M. Sidneys own iudgement, and augmented with my Obseruations, leaste we ouerthrowe one an other and be ouerthrown of the rest. . . .

(Edmund Spenser to Gabriel Harvey, April 1580: excerpt)

c. I would gladly be acquainted with M. DRANTS Prosodye, and I beseeche you commende me to good M. SIDNEYS iudgement, and gentle M. Immeritos Obseruations. I hope your nexte Letters, which I daily expect, wil bring me in farther familiaritie and acquaintance with al three. Mine owne Rules and Precepts of Arte I beleeue wil fal out not greatly repugnant, though peradventure somewhat different . . . I am of Opinion there is no one more regular and iustifiable direction, eyther for the assured and infallible Certaintie of our English Artificiall Prosodye particularly, or certainly to bring our Language into Arte and to frame a Grammer or Rhetorike thereof, than first of all uniuersally to agree upon ONE AND THE SAME ORTOGRAPHIE, in all pointes conformable and proportionate to our COMMON NATURAL PROSODYE. . . .

[poetic examples omitted] Tell me, in good sooth, doth it not too euidently appeare that this English Poet wanted but a GOOD PATTERNE before his eyes, as it might be some delicate and choyce elegant Poesie of good M. SIDNEY or M. DYERS (ouer very CASTOR and POLLUX for such and many greater matters) when this trimme geere was in hatching: Much like some GENTLEWOOMEN I coulde name in England, who by all Phisick and Physiognomie too might as well haue brought forth all goodly faire children, as they haue now some ylfauoured and deformed, had they, at the tyme of their CONCEPTION, had in sight the amiable and gallant beautifull Pictures of ADONIS, CUPIDO, GANYMEDES, or the like, which no doubt would haue wrought such deepe impression in their fantasies and imaginations, as their children, and perhappes their Childrens children too, myght haue thanked them for as long as they shall haue Tongues in their heades.

. . . But hoe I pray you, gentle sirra, a word with you more. In good sooth, and by the faith I beare to the Muses, you shal neuer haue my subscription or consent (though you should charge me wyth the authoritie of fiue hundreth Maister DRANTS) to make your *carPENter*, our *CARpenter*, an inche longer or bigger than God and his Englishe people haue made him. Is there no other Pollicie to pull downe Rhyming and set uppe Versifying but you must needes correct *Magnificat*: and againste all order of Lawe, and in despite of Custome, forcibly usurpe and tyrannize uppon a quiet company of wordes that so farre beyonde the memorie of man haue so peacably enjoyed their seueral Priuiledges and Liberties, without any disturbance or the leaste controlement? What? Is HORACES *Ars Poetica* so quite out of our Englishe Poets head that he muste haue his Remembrancer to pull hym by the sleeue, and put him in mind of *Penes usum*, and *ius*, and *norma loquendi*? [*Ars Poetica*, lines 71–72, " . . . the dictate of usage, in whose power lies the judgment of speech and the right to judge it and the standard by which to judge it."] . . . Else neuer heard I any that durst presume so much ouer the Englishe (excepting a fewe suche stammerers as haue not the masterie of their owne Tongues) as to alter the Quantitie of any one sillable, otherwise than oure common speache and generall receyued Custome woulde beare them out. Would not I laughe, thinke you, to heare MESTER IMMERITO come in baldely with his *mai-EStie, royALtie, honESTie, sciENces, faCULties, exCELlent, tavERnour, manFULly*, and a thousande the like, in steade of *MAIestie, ROYaltie, HONestie*, and so forth: And trowe you anye coulde forbeare the byting of his lippe or smyling in his Sleeue, if a iolly fellowe and greate Clarke (as it mighte be youre selfe) reading a few Verses unto him, for his owene credit and commendation, should nowe and then tell him of *barGAINeth, folLOWing, harROWing, thorOUGHly*, or the like, in steade of *BARgaineth, FOLlowing, HARrowing*, and the reste. . . . Nay, haue we not somtime, by your leaue, both the Position of the firste and Dipthong of the seconde concurring in one and the same sillable, which neuerthelesse is commonly and ought necessarily to be pronounced short? I haue nowe small time to bethink me of many examples. But what say you to to the second in *merCHAUNdise*? to the third in *covenAUNTeth*? and to the fourth in *appurtenAUNces*? Durst you auenture to make any of them long, either in Prose or in Verse? I assure you I knowe who dareth not, and *SUDdenly* feareth the displeasure of all true Englishemen if he should. Say you *sudDAINly*, if you like; by my *CERtainly* and *CERtainty* I wil not. You may perceiue by the *Premisses* (which very worde I woulde haue you note by the waye too) the Latine is no rule for us. . . .

Marry, I confesse some wordes we haue indeede, as for example *fayer*, . . . *ayer*, . . . whiche are commonly and maye indifferently be used eyther wayes. For you shal as well and as ordinarily heare *fayer* as *faire*, and *Aier* as *Aire*, and bothe alike, not onely of diuers and sundrye persons but often of the very same, otherwhiles using the one, otherwhiles the other: and so *died* or *dyde, speid* or *spide, tryed* or *tride, fyer* or *fyre, myer* or *myre*, with an infinyte companye of the same sorte, sometime *Monosyllaba*, sometime *Polysyllaba*.

To conclude . . . It is not either Position, or Dipthong, or Diastole, or anye like Grammer Schoole Deuice that doeth or can indeede either make long or short, or encrease, or diminish the number of Sillables, but onely the common allowed and receuied

PROSODYE, taken up by an universall consent of all, and continued by a generall use and Custome of all. . . . . It is the vulgare and naturall Mother PROSODYE that alone worketh the feate, as the onely supreme Foundresse and Reformer of Position, Dipthong, Orthographie, or whatsoeuer else: whose Affirmatiues are nothing worth, if she once conclude the Negatiue.

    (Gabriel Harvey to Edmund Spenser, 1580: excerpt)

d. Now, of versifying there are two sorts, the one Auncient, the other Moderne: the Auncient marked the quantitie of each silable, and according to that framed his verse; the Moderne obseruing onely number (with some regarde of the accent), the chiefe life of it standeth in that like sounding of words, which wee call Ryme. Whether of these be the most excellent, would beare many speeches. The Auncient (no doubt) more fit for Musick, both words and tune obseruing quantity, and more fit liuely to expresse diuers passions, by the low and lofty sounde of the wellweyed silable. The latter likewise, with hys Ryme, striketh a certaine musick to the eare: and, in fine, sith it dooth delight, though by another way, it obtaines the same purpose: there being in eyther sweetnes, and wanting in neither maiestie. Truely the English, before any other vulgar language I know, is fit for both sorts: for, for the Ancient, the Italian is so full of Vowels that it must euer be cumbered with *Elisions*; the Dutch so, of the other side, with Consonants, that they cannot yeeld the sweet slyding fit for a Verse; the French, in his whole language, hath not one word that hath his accent in the last silable, sauing two, called *Antepenultima*; and little more hath the Spanish: and, therefore, very gracefully may they use *Dactiles*. The English is subject to none of these defects.

    Nowe, for the ryme, though wee doe not obserue quantity, yet wee obserue the accent very precisely: which other languages eyther cannot doe or will not do so absolutely. That *Caesura*, or breathing place in the middest of the verse, neither Italian nor Spanish haue, the French, and we, almost neuer fayle of.

    (Sir Philip Sidney, *An Apology for Poetry*, 1583: excerpt)

e. . . . I will also wish yow (docile Reidar) that, or* ye cummer yow with reiding thir reulis, ye may find in your self sic a beginning of Nature as yet may put in practise in your verse many of thir foirsaidis preceptis, or euer ye sie them as they are heir set doun. For gif Nature be nocht the cheif worker in this airt, Reulis wilbe bot a band to Nature, and will mak yow within short space weary of the haill airt: quhair as, gif Nature be cheif, and bent to it, reulis will be ane help and staff to Nature. . . .

FIRST, ye man understand that all syllabis are deuydit in thrie kindes: That is, some schort, some lang, and some indifferent. Be indifferent I meane they quhilk are ather lang or short, according as ye place thame.

The forme of placeing syllables in verse is this. That your first syllabe in the lyne be short, the second lang, the thrid short, the fourt lang, the fyft short, the sixt lang, and sa furth to the end of the lyne. Alwayis tak heid that the nomber of your fete in euery lyne be euin, and nocht odde: as four, six, aucht, or ten, and not thrie, fyue, seuin, or nyne, except be it in broken verse, quhilkis are out of reul and daylie inuentit be dyuers Poetis. Bot gif ye walk ask me the reulis quhairby to knaw euerie ane of thir thre foirsaidis kyndis of syllables, I answer your eare man be the onely iudge and discerner thairof. And to proue this, I remit to the iudgement of the same, quhilk of thir two lynis following flowis best,

inTO the SEA then LUcifER upSPRANG,

in THE sea THEN luCIfer TO upSPRANG.

I doubt not bot your eare makkis you easilie to persaue that the first lyne flowis weil and the uther nathing at all. The reasoun is because the first lyne leips the reule abone written—to wit, the first fute short, the second lang, and sa furth, as I shewe before— quhair as the uther is direct contrair to the same. . . .

There is also a kynde of indifferent wordis asweill as of syllabis, albeit few in nomber. The nature quhairof is that gif ye place thame in the begynning of a lyne they are shorter by a fute nor they are gif ye place thame hinmest in the lyne, as

Sen patience I man haue perforce,
I liue in hope with patience.

Ye se there are bot aucht fete in ather of baith thir lynis abone written. The cause quhairof is that *patience* in the first lyne, in respect it is in the beginning thairof, is bot of twa fete, and in the last lyine of thrie, in respect it is the hinmest word of that lyne. To knaw and discerne thir kynde of wordis from utheris, your eare man be the onely iudge, as of all the uther parts of *Flowing*, the verie twichestane quhairof is *Musique*. . . .

> (King James VI, *Ane Schort Treatise Conteining Some Reulis and Cautelis to be Obseruit and Eschewit in Scottis Poesie*, 1584: excerpt)

---

*or = before

f. The most usuall and frequented kind of our English Poetry hath alwayes runne upon and to this day is obserued in such equall number of syllables and likenes of wordes that in all places one verse either immediatly, or by mutuall interposition, may be aunswerable to an other both in proportion of length and ending of lynes in the same Letters [i.e., rhyme]. Which rude kinde of verse, though (as I touched before) it rather discrediteth our speeche, as borrowed from the *Barbarians*, then furnisheth the same with any comely ornament, yet beeing so ingraffed by custome, and frequented by the most parte, I may not utterly dissalowe it, least I should seeme to call in question the iudgment of all our famous wryters, which haue wonne eternall prayse by theyr memorable workes compyled in that verse. . . .

There be three speciall notes necessary to be obserued in the framing of our accustomed English Ryme. The first is, that one meeter or verse be aunswerable to an other, in equall number of feete or syllables, or proportionable to the tune whereby it is to be reade or measured. The second, to place the words in such sorte as none of them be wrested contrary to the naturall inclination or affectation of the same, or more truely the true quantity thereof. The thyrd, to make them fall together mutually in Ryme, that is, in wordes of like sounde, but so as the wordes be not disordered for the Rymes sake, nor the sence hindered. . . .

The naturall course of most English verses seemeth to run uppon the olde Iambicke stroake, and I may well thinke by all likelihoode it had the beginning thereof. For if you marke the right quantitie of our usuall verses, ye shall perceiue them to containe in sound the very propertie of Iambicke feete, as thus,

i THAT my SLENder OATen PIPE in VERSE was WONT to SOUNDE.

For transpose anie of those feete in pronouncing, and make short either the two, foure, sixe, eight, tenne, twelue sillable, and it will (doo what you can) fall out very absurdly.

Againe, though our wordes can not well bee forced to abyde the touch of *Position* and other rules of *Prosodia*, yet is there such a naturall force or quantity in eche worde, that it will not abide anie place but one, without some foule disgrace: as for example try anie verse. as thys,

> *of SHAPes transFORMde to BODies STRANGE i*
> *PURpose TO inTREATE.*

Make the first sillable long, or the third, or the fift, and so forrth, or, contrariwise, make the other sillables to admitte the shortnesse of one of them places, and see what a wonderful defacing it will be to the wordes, as thus,

> *OF strange BODies TRANSformed TO shapes*
> *PURpose I to INtreate.*

So that this is one especiall thing to be taken heede of in making a good English verse, that by displacing no worde bee wrested against his naturall propriety, whereunto you shal perceyue eche worde to be affected, and may easilie discerne it in wordes of two sillables or aboue, though somme there be of indifference, that wyll stand in any place. Againe, in couching the whole sentence, the like regarde is to be had that wee exceede not too boldly in placing the verbe out of his order and too farre behind the nowne: which the necessitie of Ryme may oftentimes urge. For though it be tollerable in a verse to settle wordes so extraordinarily as other speeche will not admitt, yet heede is to be taken least by too much affecting that manner we make both the verse unpleasant and the sence obscure. . . .

The speciall poyntes of a true verse are the due obseruations of the feete and place of the feete.

The foote of a verse is a measure of two sillables, or of three, distinguished by time which is eyther long or short. A foote of two sillables is eyther simple or mixt, that is, of like time or of diuers. . . . The place of the feete is the disposing of them in

41

theyr propper roomes, whereby may be discerned the difference of eche verse which is the right numbering of the same. Now as for the quantity of our wordes, therein lyeth great difficultye, and the cheefest matter in this faculty. For in truth there being such diuersity betwixt our words and the Latine, it cannot stande indeede with great reason that they shoulde frame, wee beeing onelie directed by such rules as serue for onely Latine words; yet notwithstanding one may well perceiue by these fewe that these kinde of verses would well become the speeche, if so bee there were such Rules prescribed as woulde admitt the placing of our aptest and fullest words together. For indeede, excepting a fewe of our *Monasyllables*, which naturally should most of them be long, we haue almost none that will stand fitlie in a short foote: and therfore, if some exception were made against the precise obseruation of *Position* and certaine other of the rules, then might we haue as great plenty and choyse of good wordes to furnish and sette forth a verse as in any other tongue.

Likewise, if there were some derection in such wordes as fall not within the compasse of Greeke or Latine rules, it were a great helpe . . . I for my part, though (I must needes confesse) many faultes escaped me in these fewe, yet tooke I as good heede as I coulde, and in trueth did rather alwaies omitt the best wordes and such as would naturally become the speech best then I wolde committe any thing which shoulde notoriously impugne the Latine rules, which herein I had onely for my direction. . . .

(William Webbe, *A Discourse of English Poetrie, Together with the Authors iudgment, touching the reformation of our English Verse*, 1586)

g. Then as there was no art in the world till by experience found out: so if Poesie be now an Art, and of al antiquitie hath bene among the Greeks and Latines, and yet were none, untill by studious persons fashioned and reduced into a method of rules and precepts, then no doubt may there be the like with us. And if th'art of Poesie be but a skill appertaining to utterance, why may not the fame be with us aswel as with them, our language being no lesse copious pithie and significatiue then theirs, our conceipts the same, and our wits no lesse apt to deuise and imitate then theirs were? If againe Art be but a certaine order of rules prescribed by reason, and gathered by experience, why should not Poesie be a vulgar Art with us aswell as with the Greeks and

Latines, our language admitting no fewer rules and nice diuersities then theirs? but peraduenture moe by a peculiar, which our speech hath in many things differing from theirs: and yet in the generall points of that Art, allowed to go in common with them: so as if one point perchance which is their feete whereupon their measures stand, and in deede is all the beautie of their Poesie, and which feete we haue not, nor as yet neuer went about to frame (the nature of our language and wordes not permitting it) we haue in stead thereof twenty other curious points in that skill more then they euer had, by reason of our rime and tunable concords or simphonie, which they neuer obserued. Poesie therefore may be an Art in our vulgar [tongue], and that verie methodicall and commendable. . . .

(George Puttenham, *The Arte of English Poesie*, 1589)

10 / Elizabethan and Jacobean Poets

a.   Three variations on a theme

(1)   come LIVE/ with MEE,/ and BE/ my LOVE,/
and WE/ will ALL/ the PLEA/sures PROVE,/
that VAL/lies, GROVES/, HILLS/ and FIELDES,/
WOODS/ or STEE/pie MOUN/taine YEELDES./

and WEE/ will SIT/ upON/ the ROCKS,/   5
SEEing/ the SHEEP/heards FEEDE/ theyr
   FLOCKS/
by SHAL/low RI/vers, TO/ whose FALLS/
meLOD/ious BYRDS/ sing MAD/riGALLS./

and I/ will MAKE/ thee BEDS/ of ROses,/
AND/ a THOUS/and FRA/grant POEsies,/   10
a CAP/ of FLOW/ers, AND/ a KIRtle,/
imBROY/dred ALL/ with LEAVES/ of MIRtle./

a GOWNE/ MADE of/ the FI/nest WOOLL,/
which FROM/ our PRET/ty LAMBES/ we
   PULL,/
FAYRE lined/ SLIPpers/ FOR the/ COLD,/   15
with BUCK/les OF/ the PU/rest GOLD./

a BELT/ of STRAW/ and I/vie BUDS,/
with CO/rall CLASPS/ and AM/ber STUDS,/

44

and IF/ these PLEA/sures MAY/ thee MOVE,/
come LIVE/ with MEE,/ and BE/ my LOVE./   20

the SHEEP/heards SWAINES/ shall DAUNCE/
   and SING/
for THY/ deLIGHT/ each MAY-/morNING./
if THESE/ deLIGHTS/ thy MINDE/ may MOVE,/
then LIVE/ with MEE,/ and BE/ my LOVE./
            (Christopher Marlowe, "The Passionate
            Sheepheard to his love," 1589?)

The scansion of line three depends on (a) taking "groves" as
monosyllabic and (b) assuming that Marlowe more or less paired
off the two parts of the line ("that VAL/lies, GROVES,/" and
"HILLS/ and FIELDES,/"), thus providing a kind of natural
caesura at the exact point that perfectly balances one half of a
tetrameter line against the other. This would of course be sing-
songy if practised regularly. Marlowe flirts with that sort of
balance in line fifteen, but does not ever in fact repeat the prosody
of line three.

His fondness for counterpointing the basic iambic metric with
first-foot stresses and even an inverted iambic in the second foot
(as in line thirteen) produces what I have here scanned as a
trochaic line, in line fifteen. (The apparently similar pattern in
line ten is probably held in its iambic mold, though precariously,
by the parallisms with line nine, including the feminine end-
rhyme.) Line fifteen is not decisively trochaic: Marlowe's ear
seems frequently more fascinated by flux and tension than by
certainty. If "lined" is read bisyllabically, as I do not think it is
to be read, the line can be scanned "fayre LIN/ed SLIP/pers
FOR/ the COLD." This is not I think the correct scansion; it
does however suggest the kind of pull between alternative
rhythms that Marlowe liked to exploit.

Ralegh's prosodic practice is strikingly different:

(2) if ALL/ the WORLD/ and LOVE/ were YOUNG./
     and TRUTH/ in EVE/ry SHEEP/heards TONGUE,/
     these PRET/ty PLEA/sures MIGHT/ me MOVE,/
     to LIVE/ with THEE,/ and BE/ thy LOVE./

45

time DRIVES/ the FLOCKS/ from FIELD/ to FOLD,/   5
when RI/vers RAGE,/ and ROCKS/ grow COLD,/
and PHI/loMELL/ beCOM/meth DOMBE,/
the REST/ comPLAINES/ of CARES/ to COME./

the FLOW/ers* do FADE,/ and WAN/ton FIELDES,/
to WAY/ward WIN/ter RECK/oning† YEELDES,/   10
a HON/ny TONGUE,/ a HART/ of GALL,/
is FAN/cies SPRING, but SOR/rowes FALL./

thy GOWNES,/ thy SHOOES,/ thy BEDS/ of ROses,/
thy CAP,/ thy KIR/tle, AND/ thy POEsies,/
soone BREAKE,/ soone WI/ther, SOONE/ forGOTten:/   15
in FOL/lie RIPE,/ in REA/son ROTten./

thy BELT/ of STRAW/ and I/vie BUDDES,/
thy CO/rall CLASPES/ and AM/ber STUDDES,/
all THESE/ in ME/ no MEANES/ can MOVE,/
to COME/ to THEE,/ and BE/ thy LOVE./   20

but COULD/ youth LAST,/ and LOVE/ still BREEDE,/
had IOYES/ no DATE,/ nor AGE/ no NEEDE,/
then THESE/ deLIGHTS/ my MINDE/ might MOVE,/
to LIVE/ with THEE,/ and BE/ thy LOVE./
(Sir Walter Ralegh, "The Nimphs reply to
the Sheepheard," 1590?)

---

*monosyllabic?
†bisyllabic?

(3) come LIVE/ with MEE,/ and BEE/ my LOVE,/
and WE/ will SOME/ new PLEA/sures PROVE/
of GOL/den SANDS,/ and CHRIS/tall BROOKES,/
with SIL/ken LINES,/ and SIL/ver HOOKES./

THERE will/ the RI/ver WHISP/ering* RUNNE/   5
WARM'D by/ thy EYES,/ MORE then/ the SUNNE,/
and THERE/ the'inAM/or'd FISH/ will STAY,/
BEGging/ themSELVES/ they MAY/ beTRAY./

when THOU/ wilt SWIMME/ in THAT/ live BATH,/
each FISH,/ which EVE/ry CHAN/nell HATH,/   10

will A/moROUS/ly TO/ thee SWIMME,/
GLADder/ to CATCH/ thee, THEN/ thou HIM./

if THOU,/ to BE/ so SEENE,/ beest* LOATH,/
by SUNNE,/ or MOONE,/ thou DARK/nest BOTH,/
and IF/ my SELFE/ hath LEAVE/ to SEE,/   15
i NEED/ not THEIR/ light, HAV/ing THEE./

let O/thers FREEZE/ with AN/gling REEDS,/
and CUT/ their LEGGES,/ with SHELLS/ and WEEDS,/
or TREA/cherousLY†/ poore FISH/ beSET,/
with STRAN/gling SNARE,/ or WIN/dowie NET:/   20

let COARSE/ bold HANDS,/ from SLI/my NEST/
the BED/ded FISH/ in BANKS/ out-WREST,/
or CU/rious* TRAIT/ors, SLEAVES/like FLIES/
beWITCH/ poore FISH/es WAN/dring EYES./

for THEE,/ thou NEEDST/ no SUCH/ deCEIT,/   25
for THOU/ thy SELFE/ art THINE/ owne BAIT;/
that FISH,/ that IS/ not CATCH'D/ thereBY,/
aLAS,/ is WI/ser FARRE/ then I./
                    (John Donne, "The Baite," 1595?)
_____
*bisyllabic?
†trisyllabic?

The prosodic contrast between Donne's highwire act, full of
incredible turns and stops that just escape falling from the
heights, and the stalwart regularities of Ralegh's metrics, is as
great as the prosodic contrast between Ralegh and the dextrous,
subtle, even sly prosodic variations of Marlowe. Donne's metrics
never break down: that must be said at once. (Indeed, Ben
Jonson's strictures are not only undeserved, they in fact apply a
good deal more accurately to Jonson himself, as I will demonstrate shortly.) But the combination of, on the one hand, metrically dazzling freedoms and near-misses and, on the other, a
denseness of both metaphor and of linguistic rhythms, clearly
makes Donne's prosody unique—and uniquely difficult.
    Consider, for example, the instances in "The Baite" in which,
by convention, we scan a foot iambically, though in actual speech

(i.e., linguistically) we might just as well stress either syllable, or even both. (It is worth noting that both stress variation and the rising native movement of English are so powerful that, in truth, we cannot ever truly find a spondee—two consecutive stressed syllables within the same foot. Lines like Tennyson's "Break, break, break," which might seem to violate this proscription, are in fact three consecutive monosyllabic feet.)

/will SOME/ (line 2)
/new PLEA/sures (line 2)
/they MAY/ (line 8)
/when THOU/ (line 9)
/wilt SWIMME/ (line 9)
/live BATH/ (line 9)
/each FISH/ (line 10)
/beest LOATH/ (line 13)
/thou DARK/nest (line 14)
/haue LEAVE/ (line 15)
/poore FISH/ (line 19)
/let COARSE/ (line 21)
/bold HANDS/ (line 21)
/thou NEEDST/ (line 25)
/art THINE/ (line 26)
/owne BAIT/ (line 26)
/that FISH/ (line 27)
/that IS/ (line 27)
/then I/ (line 28)

To the nineteen items on this list we need to add those instances in which Donne pretty clearly inverts the iambic movement, though the second syllable in the foot is, linguistically, relatively strong:

/THERE will/ (line 5)
/WARM'D by/ (line 6
/MORE then/ (line 6)

And to these lists we also need to add the strange regularities of line sixteen, the eight syllables of which include seven with significant linguistic stress. Only the second syllable of "having" is a traditional unstressed syllable. As he does throughout his

48

poetry, Donne makes these idiosyncratic feet combine beautifully and harmoniously—and just how idiosyncratic they in fact are can perhaps best be seen by preparing for Ralegh's poem a list like those just set out for Donne. There is of course nothing in Ralegh's poem comparable to line sixteen of Donne's, nor are there any inverted feet. Indeed, there is a total of only four items to list, and of these three do not occur until the final stanza:

/time DRIVES/ (line 15)
/youth LAST/ (line 21)
/still BREEDE/ (line 21)
/might MOVE/ (line 23)

Ralegh's prosodic world is extraordinarily unlike Donne's. But the very degree of difference, and the fact that both poets are obviously still functioning within a set of shared operating principles and conventions, also serves to emphasize what a flexible, effective, and intensely practical prosody English had finally achieved. The superb ease with which Spenser handles prosody is still further evidence:

b.   CALME was/ the DAY,/ and THROUGH/ the
         TREM/bling AYRE,/
      sweete BREATH/ing ZE/phyRUS/ did SOFT/ly PLAY/
      a GEN/tle SPIR/it, that LIGHT/ly DID/ deLAY/
      hot TI/tans BEAMES,/ which THEN/ did
         GLYS/ter FAYRE:/
      when I/ whom SUL/lein CARE,/   5
      through DIS/conTENT/ of MY/ long FRUIT/lesse
         STAY/
      in PRIN/ces COURT,/ and EX/pecTA/tion VAYNE/
      of I/dle HOPES,/ which STILL/ doe FLY/ aWAY,/
      like EMP/ty SHAD/dowes, DID/ afFLICT/ my
         BRAYNE,/
      walkt FORTH/ to EASE/ my PAYNE/   10
      aLONG/ the SHOARE/ of SIL/uer STREA/ming
         THEMMES,/
      whose RUT/ty BANCKE,/ the WHICH/ his RI/ver
         HEMMES,/

was PAYN/ted ALL/ with VA/riAB/le FLOWERS*,/
and ALL/ the MEADES/ aDORND/ with DAIN/tie
    BOWRES,/
and CROWNE/ their PA/raMOURS,/   15
aGAINST/ the BRY/dale DAY,/ which IS/ not
    LONG:/
sweete THEMMES/ runne SOFT/ly, TILL/ i END/
    my SONG./
                (Edmund Spenser, "Prothalamion," 1596: excerpt)

---

*the rhyme suggests elision

But a century and a half of confusion, and the negative weight of
both the classical and the continental examples, did not simply
vanish overnight. In the work of sturdy but lesser poets, like
Fulke Greville, the harmonious tensions of Donne and Spenser
can still clot and curdle:

c. LOVE, the/ deLIGHT/ of ALL/ well-THIN/king
        MINDS,/
    deLIGHT,/ the FRUIT/ of VER/tue DEARE/ly
        LOV'D,/
    VERtue,/ the HIGH/est GOOD/ that REA/son FINDS,/
    REAson,/ the FIRE/ whereIN/ men's
        THOUGHTS/ bee PROV'D,/
    ARE from/ the WORLD/ by NA/ture's POWER/*
        beREFT,/   5
    and IN/ one CREA/ture, FOR/ her GLOry, LEFT./

    BEAUtie/ her CO/ver IS,/ the EYES'/ true
        PLEAsure;/
    in HO/nour's FAME/ she LIVES,/ the
        EARES'/ sweet MUsicke;/
    exCESSE/ of WON/der GROWES/ from
        HER/ true MEAsure;/
    her WORTH/ is PAS/sion's WOUND/ and
        PAS/sion's PHYsicke;/   10
    from HER/ true HEART/ cleare SPRINGS/ of
        WIS/dome FLOW,/
    which I/mag'd IN/ her WORDS/ and DEEDS,/ men
        KNOW./

time FAINE/ would STAY,/ that SHE/ might NE/ver
   LEAVE her,/
PLACE doth/ reIOYCE/ that SHE/ must NEEDS/
   conTAINE her,/
death CRAVES/ of HEA/ven that SHE/ may NOT/
   beREAVE her,/
the HEA/vens KNOW/ their OWNE/ and DOE/
   mainTAINE her;/
deLIGHT,/ love, REA/son, VER/tue LET/ it BE/
to SET/ all WO/men LIGHT,/ but ON/ly SHE./

15

         (Fulke Greville, "Caelica," Poem I: ca. 1586?)

---

*monosyllabic?

"There are times, certainly," says the editor of a recent collection of Fulke Greville's poems, "when the poet seems to be
trying to carve his verses out against the grain of language,"
adding that "there is little profit or pleasure in the process."
(Joan Rees, ed., *Selected Writings of Fulke Greville*, London,
Athlone Press, 1973, p.9) No more intellectual, surely, than
Donne, Greville plainly lacks full command of his poetic instrument. In stanza one, for example, he uses the quite ordinary and
predictable first-foot inverted iamb—but uses it in four of the
stanza's six lines, thus making the verse movement stiff and
mechanical. (Line five might be scanned "are FROM," but even
three of six is extraordinarily excessive.) In both stanzas two and
three he similarly over-uses the feminine end-rhyme, which if
employed discretely can add a pleasant off-beat to a basically
iambic metric. But to have feminine rhymes in eight of twelve
lines—indeed, in two sequences of four lines in a row—is oppres-
sive rather than enhancing. (Byron, with an infinitely better ear,
knew that a plethora of feminine rhyme tends to undercut rather
than reinforce, and uses it in exactly that way, to brilliant satiric
effect, in his comic masterpiece, *Don Juan*.) Further, too many
of Greville's prosodic feet are composed of stolid monosyllabic
words, as in the first foot of line five, the first foot of line six, the
fourth foot of line nine, the first foot of line eleven, the third foot
of lines thirteen, fourteen, and fifteen (which in fact use the same
two monosyllabic words in the same metrical position of all three
lines!), and the fourth foot of line sixteen.
    Above all, there is no sense that Greville understood either the

power or the importance of the natural speech movement of the language. Donne's frequently compressed images are set in a matrix of inevitable, unstoppable linguistic propulsion; in his verse the syntax of English sweeps constantly forward, rushing through the lines as they unroll, fairly propelling the reader on. Donne's formal metrical arrangements are, as of course they should be, harnessed to this natural speech movement. His prosodic music is not identical to the linguistic music, nor does it need to be. But the relationship is close enough so that the tension is additive rather than distractive. In Greville's first stanza, on the other hand, Latinate clause-structures smother and virtually stifle any natural linguistic movement. Stanzas one and two, and all but the last two lines of stanza three, are rhythmically end-stopped, without either the resonant, satisfying close-rhyming of the heroic couplet or indeed any sense that Greville truly understands the ornamental function of rhyme. (See, above, my remarks on Greville's abuse of feminine rhymes in stanzas two and three.)

Technically correct as they are, accordingly, Greville's iambic pentameter lines not only lack grace but seem to reflect the heritage of uncertainty and mis-metering that, as we have seen, came to a formal end with the verse of Surrey. That century and a half of confusion, still to be vividly seen in Elizabethan writing about prosody, did not endure long. But it could not be expected to dissipate, like a fog, at the first touch of the sun.

d. UNto/ the BOUND/les O/cean OF/ thy BEAUtie/
    RUNS this/ poore RI/ver, CHARG'D/ with STREAMES/
        of ZEALE:/
    reTURN/ing THEE/ the TRI/bute OF/ my DUtie,/
    which HEERE/ my LOVE,/ my YOUTH,/ my
        PLAYNTS/ reVEALE./
        HEERE i/ unCLASPE/ the BOOKE/ of MY/
        charg'd SOULE,/   5
    where I/ have CAST/ th'acCOUNTS/ of ALL/
        my CARE:/
    HEERE have/ i SUMM'D/ my SIGHES,/ HEERE
        i/ enROULE/
    HOWE they/ were SPENT/ for THEE;/ LOOKE
        what/ they ARE./

LOOKE on/ the DEERE/ exPEN/ses OF/ my
    YOUTH,/
and SEE/ how IUST/ i REC/kon WITH/ thyne
    EYES:/   10
exAM/ine WELL/ thy BEAU/tie WITH/ my
    TRUETH*,/
and CROSSE/ my CARES/ ere GREA/ter SUMMES/
    aRISE./
READE it,/ sweet MAIDE,/ though IT/ be
    DOONE/ but SLIGHTly;/
WHO can/ shew ALL/ his LOVE,/ doth LOVE/ but
    LIGHTly./
                  (Samuel Daniel, "Delia," sonnet I, 1592)

*monosyllabic, to rhyme with "youth"

The sense of *playing* with, and against, the natural movement of
English is exuberantly clear. Daniel was the son of a musician;
his ear is delicately tuned. Prosodic variations are tied to syntax
and sense—and nothing is heavy or excessive.

e.   that TIME/ of YEEARE/ thou MAIST/ in ME/
        beHOLD,/
    when YEL/low LEAVES,/ or NONE,/ or FEW/ doe
        HANGE/
    upON/ those BOUGHES/ which SHAKE/
        aGAINST/ the COULD,/
    bare RU/in'd QUIERS,/ where LATE/ the SWEET/ birds
        SANG./
    in ME/ thou SEEST/ the TWI/-light OF/ such DAY/   5
    as AF/ter SUN/-set FA/deth IN/ the WEST,/
    which BY/ and BY/ blacke NIGHT/ doth TAKE/ aWAY,/
    death's SE/cond SELF/ that SEALS/ up ALL/ in REST./
    in ME/ thou SEEST/ the GLOW/ing OF/ such FIRE/
    that ON/ the ASH/es OF/ his YOUTH/ doth LYE,/   10
    AS the/ DEATH bed,/ whereON/ it MUST/ exPIRE,/
    conSUM'D/ with THAT/ which IT/ was NUR/risht BY./
        this THOU/ perCEV'ST,/ which MAKES/ thy
            LOVE/ more STRONG,/
        to LOVE/ that WELL,/ which THOU/ must
            LEAVE/ ere LONG./
              (William Shakespeare, Sonnet 73, ca. 1595)

Like Donne, Shakespeare exploited both the prosodic scheme and the natural movement of the language, setting them now in tune, now in strong counterpoint, with unparalleled deftness. The stunning trochaic intrusion in the first two feet of line eleven is strikingly effective. Note that there are almost two dozen instances, in this fourteen-line poem, where (apart from wholly monosyllabic feet like "in ME" and "or NONE") the balance between the two syllables of the foot is linguistically close. Many of these are resolvable only by convention, like "bare RU/in'd" in line four or "more STRONG" in line thirteen. As with Donne, so high an incidence of linguistically marginal stress choices is evidence of how tautly the poet exploits the tension between linguistic and metrical readings. (Although rhyme is not the subject of this book, I cannot help drawing attention to the emphatic way in which Shakespeare tosses off "by and by" in line seven, only to return to [ay] as his rhyme-sound in lines ten and twelve. In a rhyme-poor language like English, this is a delicately swaggering touch that adds to the bravura nature of the poem: it is as if the poet had declared, "See? My rhyming is so effortless that I can waste this rhyme-sound, then waste it yet again—and still use it as a rhyme-sound just a few lines further along.")

f.   my MI/stres EYES/ are NO/thing LIKE/ the SUNNE,
       CUrall/ is FARRE/ more RED,/ then HER/ lips RED,/
       if SNOW/ be WHITE,/ why THEN/ her BRESTS/ are
           DUN:/
       if HAIRES/ be WIERS,/ black WIERS/ GROW on/ her
           HEAD:/
       I have/ seene RO/ses DA/maskt, RED/ and WHITE,/   5
       but NO/ such RO/ses SEE/ i IN/ her CHEEKES,/
       AND in/ some PER/fumes IS/ there MORE/ deLIGHT,/
       THEN in/ the BREATH/ that FROM/ my MI/stres
           REEKES./
       i LOVE/ to HEARE/ her SPEAKE,/ yet WELL/ i
           KNOW/
       that MU/sicke HATH/ a FARRE/ more PLEA/sing
           SOUND:/   10
       i GRAUNT/ i NE/ver SAW/ a GOD/dess GOE,/

> my MI/stres WHEN/ she WALKES,/ TREADS
>   on/ the GROUND./
> and YET/ by HEA/ven i THINKE/ my LOVE/ as
>   RARE/
> as A/ny SHE/ beLI'D/ with FALSE/ comPARE./
> (William Shakespeare, Sonnet 130)

Lines seven and eight may not be meant to begin with reverse
iambs, as here scanned, but I do not think six can be scanned
differently. Note that lines four and twelve reverse the fourth
foot—a somewhat unusually high incidence of variation at this
position in the iambic pentameter line.

g. how MA/ny PAL/try, FOO/lish, PAIN/ted THINGS,/
   that NOW/ in COA/ches TROU/ble EV'/ry STREET,/
   shall BE/ forGOT/ten, WHOM/ no PO/et SINGS,/
   ere THEY/ be WELL/ wrap'd IN/ their WIN/ding
      SHEET?/
   where I/ to THEE/ eTER/niTIE/ shall GIVE,/   5
   when NO/thing ELSE/ reMAY/neth OF/ these DAYS,/
   and QUEENES/ hereAF/ter SHALL/ be GLAD/ to LIVE/
   upON/ the ALMES/ of THY/ suPER/fluous* PRAYSE;/
   VIRgins/ and MA/trons REA/ding THESE/ my RIMES,/
   shall BE/ so MUCH/ deLIGHT/ed WITH/ thy STOry,/   10
   that THEY/ shall GRIEVE,/ they LIV'D/ not IN/ these
      TIMES,/
   to HAVE/ seene THEE,/ their SEX/es ONE/ly GLOry:/
      so SHALT/ thou FLYE/ aBOVE/ the VUL/gar
         THRONG,/
      STILL to/ surVIVE/ in MY/ imMOR/tall SONG./
(Michael Drayton, Sonnet 5, 1594)

---

*elided?

Drayton's editor, John Buxton, remarks that, "as he knew himself," Drayton was "often 'rugged and filed,' the opposite of
Shakespeare's 'fine-filed phrase'." (John Buxton, ed., *Poems of
Michael Drayton*, Cambridge, Mass., Harvard University Press,
1953, vol. I, p.xiv) There is no truly satisfactory scansion of line
four, nor is line twelve much clearer. But there can be no doubt
that, unlike Wyatt, Drayton at least knew what he wanted to do,

prosodically speaking, though he may not have always done either as he ought or as he wanted to.

h.　SPRING, the/ sweet SPRING,/ is the YEARE'S/
　　　　pleasant KING,/
　　　then BLOOMS/ each THING,/ then maids DANCE/
　　　　in a RING,/
　　　COLD doth/ not STING,/ the pretty BIRDS/ do
　　　　SING:/
　　　　cucKOO,/ jug-JUG,/ pu-WE,/ to-WIT/ta-WOO!/

　　　the PALM/ and MAY/ make COUN/try HOU/ses
　　　　GAY,/　　　　　　　　　　　　　　　　　　　5
　　　lambs FRISK/ and PLAY,/ the SHEP/herds PIPE/ all
　　　　DAY,/
　　　and WE/ heare AYE/ birds TUNE/ this MER/ry
　　　　LAY:/
　　　　cucKOO,/ jug-JUG,/ pu-WE,/ to-WIT/ta-WOO!/

　　　the FIELDES/ breathe SWEET,/ the DAI/sies KISS/
　　　　our FEET,/
　　　young LO/vers MEET,/ old WIVES/ a-SUN/ning
　　　　SIT,/　　　　　　　　　　　　　　　　　　　10
　　　in EV/'ry STREET/ these TUNES/ our
　　　　EARS/ do GREET:/
　　　　cucKOO,/ jug-JUG,/ pu-WE,/ to-WIT/ta-WOO!/
　　　　　SPRING, the/ sweet SPRING!/
　　　(Thomas Nashe, "Spring, the Sweet Spring," 1592)

This is a song from a play, *Summer's Last Will and Testament.* Since the form is replicative, as the presence of a refrain emphasizes, we would expect the metric of each stanza to be the same. (Since formal patterns can be relevant to metrical patterns, it is usually better not to definitively scan virtually any line in a poem, and especially the first few lines, until the whole poem has been scanned.) The rather mechanical internal rhyming of the second and the last stress in each line, as well as the use of only a single rhyme-sound in all six rhyming positions, in all three stanzas, further emphasizes this formal repetition. ("Sit" is of course not a perfect rhyme for "feet," though [iy] was probably not pronounced quite so long, in Elizabethan England, as it is today.) There is no doubt that the first three lines of stanzas two and three are iambic pentameter, as is the refrain in all three stanzas. The second and third lines of the first stanza can be read as pentameter, though not gracefully:

> then BLOOMS/ each THING,/ then MAIDS/ DANCE in/
>   a RING,/
> COLD doth/ not STING,/ the PRET/ty BIRDS/ do SING./

This scansion is about as likely, or as unlikely, as that noted above for these lines. The problem is that line one, though it contains the ten syllables that are one requirement (give or take a syllable or two) of iambic pentameter, falls almost infallibly into four rather than five linguistic and metrical stresses. There is the extremely doubtful possibility of placing metrical stress on "sweet": "SPRING/ the SWEET/ SPRING is/ the YEARE'S/ pleasant KING./" Not only is this no improvement over the tetrameter scansion, above, but it breaks the clear pattern, throughout the nine principal lines of the poem, of having the caesura between feet two and three. It also interferes awkwardly with the internal rhyming that is so strong a formal feature of these same lines. Similarly strong objections can be made to placing metrical stress on either "is" or the first syllable of "pleasant." Since it seems to make better (if not good) sense to scan the three principal lines of the first stanza in the same prosodic measure, and since, although line one pretty stubbornly resist anything but a tetrameter scansion, lines two and three can be scanned about equally well (or poorly) as pentameter or tetrameter, I have with some hesitation suggested tetrameter scansions for lines one through three. I have no great confidence in this proposal—for it seems to me that there is pretty clearly a metrically uncertain ear at work in this poem. Nashe is of course better known for his prose. More: the fact that this was the verbal text for a performed piece of music indicates not only the shaping effect of an unknown melody or melodies, and possibly even of some form of choreography, but also assorted other nonliterary and nonwritten influences. The comparative technical clumsiness of the poem as a whole further underlines the probability that Sir Philip Sidney's work is not the primary model for Nashe's poem. There is no evidence of even debased Old English-style alliteration: we have no way of knowing exactly why Nashe does what he does.

But the significant thing, simply stated, is that he in fact does it. That is, to generalize on the basis of this and other indications of imperfect scansion, it would seem that command of the Chaucerian Compromise remained something less than perfect until that metrical standard began to loosen its hold on the English-language poetic world.

i.   WOULD'ST/ thou HEARE,/ what MAN/ can SAY/
     IN/ a LIT/tle? REA/der, STAY./
     UN/der-NEATH/ this STONE/ doth LYE/
     AS/ much BEAU/tie, AS/ could DYE:/
     WHICH/ in LIFE/ did HAR/bour GIVE/   5
     TO/ more VER/tue, THEN/ doth LIVE./
     IF,/ at ALL,/ shee HAD/ a FAULT,/
     LEAVE/ it BU/ryed IN/ this VAULT./
     ONE/ name WAS/ eLI/zaBETH,/
     TH'OTH/er LET/ it SLEEPE/ with DEATH:/   10
     FIT/ter, WHERE/ it DYED,/ to TELL,/
     THAN that/ it LIV'D/ at ALL./ fareWELL./
                          (Ben Jonson, "Epitaph on
                          Elizabeth, L.H.," before 1616)

Only the twelfth and final line breaks the formal prosodic pattern, and only it has eight rather than seven syllables. This was clearly a difficult pattern for Jonson to maintain (and would be even more difficult to scan as trochaic tetrameter): he does not always keep easily or smoothly to the prosodic track. The almost unvarying metrical stress on the first syllable in each line is barely, not to say awkwardly, sustained. The first three lines, indeed, seem better suited to a loose trimeter: their natural linguistic movement stresses "hear," "Man," and "say," in line one; the first syllable of "little" and "reader" and "stay," in line two; and the final syllable of "underneath" as well as "stone" and "lie," in line three. Stress on "as" rather than on "much" in line four butts hard against both the natural linguistic facts and the poetic convention which, as we have seen, metrically stresses the second syllable in a foot when there is no way otherwise to choose between it and the first syllable. Jonson's supervening pattern of first-syllable stress is a slender reed for a poet to stand on, here, considering especially the greater linguistic weight of "much." The metrical stress on "to" rather than "more," in line five, seems even more forced and ineffective. Only a rhetorical twist allows Jonson to stress "one" rather than "name," in line nine. In sum, the distance between linguistic stress and metrical stress, as so often in Jonson, is abnormally high. Rather than exploiting tension and pull between the two standards, Jonson comes perilously close to separating them, thus making of the metrical standard an arbitrary and nonlinguistic thing.

I have already referred to Jonson's heavy, and frequently clumsy, reliance on the prosodic apostrophe. Line ten provides an excellent example. One of Jonson's best and most famous poems, also an epitaph and again in twelve lines, provides another, as well as an example of Jonson's handling of iambic pentameter in a non-couplet form.

j. fareWELL,/ thou CHILD/ of MY/ right HAND,/ and JOY;/
my SINNE/ was TOO/ much HOPE/ of THEE,/ lov'd BOY:/
seven YEERES/ tho'wert LENT/ to ME,/ and I/ thee PAY,/
exACT/ed BY/ thy FATE,/ ON the/ just DAY./
O, could/ i LOOSE/ all FA/ther, NOW./ for WHY/ 5
will MAN/ laMENT/ the STATE/ he SHOULD/ enVIE?/
to HAVE/ so SOONE/ scap'd WORLDS,/ and FLE/shes RAGE,/
AND, if/ no O/ther MI/serIE,/ yet AGE?/
REST in/ soft PEACE,/ and, ASK'D,/ say HERE/ doth LYE/
Ben. JON/son HIS/ best PIECE/ of PO/eTRIE./ 10
FOR/ whose SAKE,/ hence-FORTH,/ all his VOWES/ be SUCH,/
as WHAT/ he LOVES/ may NE/ver LIKE/ too MUCH./
   (Ben Jonson, "On my first Sonne," 1603?)

59

Line eleven is scannable, but just barely. The awkwardly trisyllabic fourth foot is echoed by the equally awkward trisyllabic first foot of line three; yet another trisyllabic foot is avoided in the second foot of that same line only by use of the prosodic apostrophe. It is typical of Jonson's frequent prosodic clumsiness to have two such incidents occurring in successive feet: irregularities that might pass relatively unnoticed, if more spread out, become exceedingly obvious when thus concentrated. The fourth foot of line four, scanned here as "ON the," could as easily be reversed; "just DAY," in the next foot of the same line, employs a convention to overcome the somewhat great linguistic stress on "just." Again, the juxtaposition of two awkwardnesses emphasizes both. The first foot of line five, and the first foot of line eight, could as well be reversed: "o COULD" and "and IF" are as justifiable as the scansions here given. The forwarding thrust of English accent, as a matter of linguistic history, had already made "envy" an unlikely candidate for a stress on the second syllable, but there is evidence that this was still an available (if not a favored) pronunciation. Once more, Jonson has to push a bit to make his scansion fall into place.

All of which emphasizes Jonson's most peculiar claim that he was a "classical" poet and devoted to regularity and rules, while his good friend Donne was poetically licentious and ought, indeed, to be hung for "not keeping of the accent." As so often happens, subsequent critics have listened to Jonson's accusation rather than to his prosody, and have been violent and inaccurate in their judgment of Donne. This is not the place to rehearse the controversy; let me simply quote from a once-standard text, Emile Legouis and Louis Cazamian's *A History of English Literature*:

> Never has English metre, the heroic metre, suffered as at his [Donne's] hands. He wrote so-called couplets, but allowed himself to drag the sense from one line to the next in the most violent way and to make the most singular divisions of his line. More than this, he violates the iambic rhythm over and over again and many of his lines cannot be scanned.

> If all things be in all,
> As I think, since all which were, are and shall
> Be, be made of the same elements,
> Each thing each thing implies or represents.

When he rhymes unaccented syllables—offiCERS, suitORS—
the fact may be ascribed to archaism, but with little probability,
since he aimed at modernism and a reproduction of the inflections
of everyday speech. *It is rather that he despised the laws of
versification.*

(N.Y., Macmillan, 1929, pp.333–34; emphasis added)

The poem quoted, Donne's fifth Satire, is indeed a free, rollicking
blast, beginning (and unlike Legouis and Cazamian I will quote
and scan at once) "thou SHALT/ not LAUGH/ in THIS/ leafe,
MUSE,/ nor THEY/ // whom A/ny PIT/ty WARMES." The
passage quoted begins in the middle of line nine; it is free but
hardly unscannable. "if ALL/ things BE/ in ALL,/ // as I/ thinke,
since ALL,/ which WERE,/ ARE,/ and SHALL/ // BEE,/ be
MADE/ of THE/ same E/leMENTS:/ // each THING,/ each
THING/ imPLIES/ or RE/preSENTS./ //" This scansion requires
a trisyllabic foot ("thinke, since ALL"), a foot of lowly monosyllables ("of THE") and, perhaps most licentiously of all, two
monosyllabic feet, composed of forms of the copulative verb
"be." But Ben Jonson's "Epitaph on Elizabeth L.H.," quoted,
scanned, and discussed earlier, contains an abundance of monosyllabic feet, and Jonson's "On my first Sonne," also discussed
above, similarly features a trisyllabic foot. Both Jonson poems
have an unusually high number of feet composed of two monosyllables—sometimes, as noted, in distinctly odd juxtaposition.
Donne's "The Baite," a much more distinctly lyrical poem,
shows many fewer irregularities than we find in Jonson's work.
And other lyrical poems of Donne provide abundant confirma-
tion:

k.   BATter/ my HEART,/ three PER/son'd GOD;/ for
        YOU/
        as YET/ but KNOCKE,/ breathe, SHINE,/ and
        SEEKE/ to MEND;/
        that I/ may RISE,/ and STAND,/ o'erTHROW/
        mee,'and BEND/
        your FORCE,/ to BREAKE,/ blowe, BURN/ and
        MAKE/ me NEW./
        i, LIKE/ an U/surpt TOWNE,/ to'anO/ther DUE,/   5
        LAbour/ to'adMIT/ you, BUT/ oh, TO/ no END,/

61

REAson/ your VICE/roy in MEE/ mee SHOULD/
    deFEND,/
BUT/ is CAP/tiv'd, AND/ proves WEAKE/ or
    unTRUE./
yet DEARE/ly'i LOVE/ you'and WOULD/ be
    LOV/ed FAINE,/
but AM/ beTROTH'D/ unTO/ your E/neMIE:/   10
diVORCE/ mee,'unTIE,/ or BREAKE/ that
    KNOT/ aGAINE,/
TAKE mee/ to YOU,/ imPRI/son MEE, for I/
exCEPT/ you'enTHRALL/ mee, NE/ver SHALL/ be
    FREE,/
nor E/ver CHAST,/ exCEPT/ you RA/vish MEE./
        (John Donne, Holy Sonnet XIV, before 1633)

(Note how line eleven proves yet again, if proof were needed, that prosodic scansion was not intended to be governed by punctuation. That is, it was clearly understood, among poets at least, that punctuation was outside prosodic rules.) Donne here rivals Jonson in his use of the prosodic apostrophe; he also exceeds Jonson, for all that, in his lyrical ability. As Swinburne— a poet with as delicately tuned an ear as English has ever seen— observed, regretfully, "Ben . . . was one of the singers who could not sing." (Algernon Charles Swinburne, *A Study of Ben Jonson*, 1889)

l.   wilt THOU/ forGIVE/ that SINNE/ where I/ beGUNNE,/
        which WAS/ my SIN,/ though IT/ were DONE/
        beFORE?/
   wilt THOU/ forGIVE/ that SINNE,/ through WHICH/ i
        RUNNE,/
        and DO/ run STILL:/ though STILL/ i DO/
        dePLORE?/
            when THOU/ hast DONE,/ thou HAST/
        not DONE,/   5
                for I/ have MORE./

   wilt THOU/ forGIVE/ that SINNE/ which I/ have
        WONNE/
        Others/ to SINNE?/ and MADE/ my SINNE/
        their DOORE?/

wilt THOU/ forGIVE/ that SINNE/ which I/ did
    SHUNNE/
  a YEARE,/ or TWO:/ but WAL/lowed IN,/ a
    SCORE?/   10
      when THOU/ hast DONE,/ thou HAST/
    not DONE,/
           for I/ have MORE./

i HAVE/ a SINNE/ of FEARE,/ that when I/ have
    SPUNNE/
  MY last/ THRED, i/ shall PE/rish ON/ the
    SHORE;/
but SWEARE/ by thy SELFE,/ that AT/ my DEATH/ thy
    SONNE/   15
  shall SHINE/ as HE/ shines NOW,/ and
    HERE/toFORE;/
      and, HA/ving DONE/ that, THOU/
    hast DONE,/
          i FEARE/ no MORE./
(John Donne, "A Hymne to God the Father," before 1633)

m.   a SWEET/ diSOR/der IN/ the DRESSE/
      KINdles/ in CLOATHES/ a WAN/toNNESSE:/
      a LAWNE/ aBOUT/ the SHOUL/ders THROWN/
      INto/ a FINE/ disTRAC/tiON:/
      an ER/ring LACE,/ which HERE/ and THERE/   5
      enTHRALLS/ the CRIM/son STO/maCHER:/
      a CUFFE/ neGLECT/ful, AND/ thereBY/
      RIBbands/ to FLOW/ conFU/sedLY:/
      a WIN/ning WAVE/ (deSER/ving NOTE)/
      IN the/ temPES/tuous PET/tiCOTE:/   10
      a CARE/lesse SHOOE/-string, IN/ whose TYE/
      i SEE/ a WILDE/ ciVI/liTIE:/
      doe MORE/ beWITCH/ me, THEN/ when ART/
      is TOO/ preCISE/ in EVE/ry PART./
      Robert Herrick, "Delight in Disorder," before 1648)

n.   lord, HOW/ can MAN/ preach THY/ eTER/nall WORD?/
      HE is/ a BRIT/tle CRA/zie GLASSE:/
  YET in/ thy TEM/ple THOU/ dost HIM/ afFORD/

this GLO/rious AND/ tranSCEND/ent
PLACE,/
to BE/ a WIN/dow, THROUGH/ thy
GRACE./   5
but WHEN/ thou DOST/ anNEAL/ in GLASSE/ thy
STOrie,/
MAking/ thy LIFE/ to SHINE/ withIN/
the HO/ly PREA/chers; THEN/ the LIGHT/ and
GLOrie/
more REV/'rend GROWS,/ and
MORE/ doth WIN:/
which ELSE/ shows WA/trish, BLEAK,/
and THIN./   10

DOCtrine/ and LIFE,/ COlours/ and LIGHT,/ in ONE/
when THEY/ comBINE/ and
MIN/gle, BRING/
a STRONG/ reGARD/ and AWE:/ but SPEECH/
aLONE/
doth VA/nish LIKE/ a FLA/ring THING,/
and IN/ the EARE,/ not CON/science
RING./   15
(George Herbert, "The Windows," before 1633)

We might expect a stress, both linguistic and prosodic, on the
first word, "Lord." But the poem's replicative form makes it
clear that the first line of each stanza must be iambic pentameter,
and a prosodic stress on "Lord" can produce a pentameter line
only by wrenching other things about: "LORD, how/ can MAN/
preach THY/ eTER/nal WORD?/" The hopping, skipping first
two feet would be awkward in the extreme, here; further, the line
being a syntactically complete interrogative, the opposition of
"man" and "thy" fairly requires a stress, both linguistic and
prosodic, on "HOW." The first foot of line two may be reversed,
as here scanned, or may not: there is no way to be sure. The
stress on "thy" in line neither requires nor produces a similar
stress on "thy" in line three: mere repetition is not syntactic
parallelism, which might impose different requirements. Ditto
line seven, where "thy" is again unstressed. Line eleven is
euphonious but metrically highly irregular—virtually a leitmotif

in Herbert's poetry. The first foot of line fifteen might be reversed; again, there is no way to be sure.

o.   i STRUCK/ the BOARD,/ and CRY'D,/ no MORE./
                  i WILL/ aBROAD./
      WHAT? shall/ i E/ver SIGH/ and PINE?/
    my LINES/ and LIFE/ are FREE:/ FREE as/ the
      RODE,/
      LOOSE as/ the WINDE,/ as LARGE/ as
      STORE./   5
           shall I/ be STILL/ in SUIT?/
    have I/ no HAR/vest BUT/ a THORN/
    to LET/ me BLOOD,/ and NOT/ reSTORE/
    what I/ have LOST/ with COR/diall FRUIT?/
           sure THERE/ was WINE/   10
    beFORE/ my SIGHS/ did DRIE/ it: THERE/ was
      CORN/
           beFORE/ my TEARS/ did DROWN it./
    IS the/ yeare ONE/ly LOST/ to ME?/
           have I/ no BAYES/ to CROWN it?/
    no FLOW/ers, no GAR/lands GAY?/ all BLASted?/   15
      all WASted?/
    not SO,/ my HEART:/ but THERE/ is FRUIT,/
           and THOU/ hast HANDS./
    reCO/ver ALL/ thy SIGH-/blown AGE/
    on DOU/ble PLEA/sures: LEAVE/ thy COLD/
      disPUTE/   20
    of WHAT/ is FIT,/ and NOT./ forSAKE/ thy CAGE,/
           thy ROPE/ of SANDS,/
    which PET/tie THOUGHTS/ have MADE,/ and
      MADE/ to THEE/
    good CA/ble TO/ enFORCE/ and DRAW,/
           and BE/ thy LAW,/   25
    while THOU/ didst WINK/ and WOULDST/ not
      SEE./
           aWAY;/ take HEED:/
           i WILL/ aBROAD./
    call IN/ thy DEATHS/ head THERE:/ tie UP/
      thy FEARS./
           HE that/ forBEARS/   30

to SUIT/ and SERVE/ his NEED,/
deSERVES/ his LOAD./
BUT as/ i RAV'D/ and GREW/ more FIERCE/ and
WILDE/
at EVE/ry WORD,/
me THOUGHTS/ i HEARD/ one CALL/ing,
CHILD!/   35
and I/ rePLY'd,/ my LORD./
(George Herbert, "The Collar," before 1633)

Lines two and twenty-eight are here scanned "i WILL" because, in Herbert's time, the word "will" expressed very clear volition, more like today's "I want" or the German "ich will'." If this is deliberate parallelism with similar but not identical constructions, then lines six, seven, fourteen, and perhaps line nine, might well be scanned the same way. Line thirteen is problematical: Herbert's line indentations point toward a tetrameter line, here, rather than the trimeter line that would seem more natural: "is the YEARE/ onely LOST/ to ME?/" On the other hand, line sixteen seems to be indented so as to match it up with the other dimeter lines, but is very difficult to scan as anything but monometer, especially since a dimeter scansion would break the apparent parallelism with "all BLASted" in the line immediately preceding. Still, "ALL/WASted/" would preserve the correlation between indentation and prosody, observed throughout the rest of the poem. It would be an unusual though it is not an impossible scansion.

In spite of the natural tendency to equate Herbert's soaringly positive and self-possessed substance with the techniques used to convey that substance, Joseph H. Summers' comment seems singularly apt: "The poems evince a metrical virtuosity which makes Herbert the most consistently interesting experimenter in the English lyric between Sidney and Yeats." (Joseph H. Summers, ed., George Herbert, *Selected Poetry*, N.Y., Signet/NAL, 1967, p.xxvi)

11 / Milton, Marvell, and Vaughan

a. NOW the/ bright MOR/ning STAR,/ dayes HAR/binGER,/
comes DAN/cing FROM/ the EAST,/ and LEADS/ with
HER/
the FLOW/ry MAY,/ who FROM/ her GREEN/ lap
THROWS/
the YEL/low COW/slip, AND/ the PALE/ primROSE./
hail BOUN/teous MAY,/ that DOST/ inSPIRE/   5
MIRTH/ and YOUTH,/ and WARM/ deSIRE,/
WOODS/ and GROVES/ are OF/ thy DRESsing,/
HILL/ and DALE/ doth BOAST/ thy BLESsing./
THUS we/ salUTE/ thee WITH/ our EAR/ly SONG,/
and WEL/com THEE,/ and WISH/ thee LONG./   10
         (John Milton, "Song: On May Morning," 1630)

Four lines of iambic pentameter are followed by four lines,
indented, of iambic tetrameter, and finally by a couplet the first
line of which is pentameter, the second (though it is not indented)
tetrameter. Considerable violence to natural word stress is required, in order to make this metrical scansion effective. All that
saves Milton is the fact that, as we have seen, metrical stress is
relative and confined to a particular foot: nothing else could keep
us from stressing both "bright" and "morning," in line one. In
speech, too, there would be a pronounced tendency to minimize
the second stress in "harbinger": in usual linguistic terms, the
first syllable of "harbinger" receives either a primary or a secondary stress, the middle syllable receives weak stress, and the

final syllable receives tertiary (not very marked) stress. Here, however, that weak stress is matched exclusively against the tertiary stress, and the prosodic convention allows us to give a jot more metrical stress to the first syllable of "harbinger" than to "dayes." If it were not for the requirement that it rhyme with /binGER/, similarly, the last foot in line two, "/with HER,/" might well be scanned "WITH her."

Milton employs these fairly wrenching principles throughout, metrically stressing "green" and "throws," in line three, but not stressing "lap," which is of the same linguistic stress; stressing "and" but not "the" in line four (and taking advantage of a still shiftable accent to stress the second rather than the first syllable of "primrose"); stressing the first syllable of "bounteous" rather than "hail," in line five (though this is not entirely certain); and stressing "of" rather than "are," in line seven.

b. what SLEN/der YOUTH/ beDEW'D/ with LI/quid
      Odours/
    COURTS thee/ on RO/ses IN/ some PLEA/sant
      CAVE,/
      PYRrha?/ for WHOM/ binds THOU/
      in WREATHS/ thy GOL/den HAIR,/
    PLAIN in/ thy NEAT/ness? O/ how OFT/ shall HE/   5
    on FAITH/ and CHANG/ed GODS/ comPLAIN:/ and
      SEAS/
      ROUGH with/ black WINDS/ and STORMS/
      unWON/ted SHALL/ adMIRE:/
    who NOW/ enJOYES/ thee CRE/duLOUS,/ all GOLD,/
    who AL/wayes VA/cant, AL/wayes A/miAble/   10
      HOPES thee,/ of FLAT/tering GALES/
      unMIND/full. HAP/less THEY/
    to WHOM/ thou unTRY'D/ seemst FAIR./ ME in/ my
      VOW'D/
    PICture/ the SA/cred WALL/ deCLARES/ t'have HUNG/
    my DANK/ and DROP/ping WEEDS/   15
      TO the/ stern GOD/ of SEA./
          (John Milton, "The Fifth Ode of Horace, Book I,
                1646–48?)

Milton's preliminary note to this translation explains, "*Quis multa gracilis te puer in rosa* render'd almost word for word without rime according to the Latin measure, as near as the Language will permit." To ensure comparison with the original, indeed, Milton printed the Latin text as well. But without any more wrenching about than in the first poem of Milton, above, this translation fits perfectly well into the English iambic pattern, which inevitably supersedes (as Milton seems to have known but did not want to admit) the literally impossible quantitative metric of Latin. Two additional small but potent indications point to Milton's resigned acceptance of reality: he employs the English prosodic apostrophe in line fourteen, and in line sixteen carefully employs non-idiomatic English phrasing, "the stern God of Sea" (rather than the idiomatic "God of the Sea"), in order to preserve the iambic pattern—though he declares he is not following that pattern at all.

c. no MORE/ of TALK/ where GOD/ or AN/gel GUEST/
with MAN,/ as WITH/ his FRIEND,/ faMI/liar US'D/
to SIT/ inDUL/gent, AND/ with HIM/ parTAKE/
RUral/ rePAST, perMIT/ting HIM/ the WHILE/
VEnial/ disCOURSE/ unBLAM'D;/ i NOW/ must CHANGE/ ₅
those NOTES/ to TRA/gic—FOUL/ disTRUST,/ and
   BREACH/
disLOY/al ON/ the PART/ of MAN,/ reVOLT/
and DI/soBE/dience*: ON/ the PART/ of HEAV'N/
now A/lienAT/ed, DIS/tance AND/ disTASTE,/
ANger/ and JUST/ reBUKE,/ and JUDGE/ment GIV'N,/ 10
that BROUGHT/ INto/ this WORLD/ a WORLD/ of WOE,/
SIN and/ her SHA/dow DEATH,/ and MI/serIE,/
death's HAR/binGER./ sad TASK,/ yet AR/guMENT/
not LESS/ but MORE/ heRO/ic THEN/ the WRATH/
of STERN/ aCHIL/les ON/ his FOE/ purSU'D/ 15
thrice FU/giTIVE/ aBOUT/ troy WALL;/ or RAGE/
of TUR/nus FOR/ laVIN'ia DI/sesPOUS'D,/
or NEP/tune's IRE/ or JU/no's, THAT/ so LONG/
perPLEX'D/ the GREEK/ and CY/therE/a's SON:/
if AN/swerAB/le STYLE/ i CAN/ obTAIN/ 20
of MY/ ceLES/tial PA/troNESS,/ who DEIGNES/
her NIGHT/ly VI/siTA/tion UN/imPLOR'D,/

and DIC/tates TO/ me SLUM/bering†, OR/ inSPIRES/
EAsie/ my UN/preME/diTA/ted VERSE/ . . .
(John Milton, *Paradise Lost*, Book IX, lines 1–24, before 1667)

---

*-dience = monosyllabic
†-bering = monosyllabic

For Milton, this is almost docilely tame iambic pentameter verse. In Book One, e.g., he has lines like "Of Thammuz yearly wounded: the Love-Tale" (line 452), which scan only with truly serious wrenching about: "of THAM/muz YEAR/ly WOUND/ ed; the LOVE/-TALE/". Or line 562 of Book One: "Thir painful steps o're the burnt soyl; and now," which can only be scanned by a similarly violent disturbance of either metrical pattern or language pattern: "thir PAIN/ful STEPS/ o're the BURNT/ SOYL;/ and NOW/". In line 756 of Book One Milton reverses the fifth and final foot, which is almost unprecedented: "at PAN/ daeMO/niUM,/ the HIGH/ CApitol/". In line 735 he does something similar: "and SAT/ as PRIN/ces, WHOM/ the suPREME/ KING/" — though it may have been permissible, in Milton's day, to pronounce the penultimate word "SUpreme," a stress shift which would regularize the line.

Milton was notoriously restive in matters technical, unhappy about rhyme (which he called in the prefatory comments to *Paradise Lost* "the Invention of a barbarous Age, to set off wretched matter and lame Meeter"), constantly striving for a range of effects which ensured, willy-nilly, that in his later verse there are "a large number of lines which are prosodically more difficult than all but a few lines of *Paradise Lost*." (Edward Weismiller, "The 'Dry' and 'Rugged' Verse," in *The Lyric and Dramatic Milton*, ed. Joseph H. Summers, N.Y., Columbia University Press, 1965, p.116). We cannot do better, I suggest, than Robert Martin Adams' formulation: "But if one concedes to Milton great technical competence in the writing of metrical stuff, some of the peculiar qualities of his verse may be associated with its largeness and boldness of assertion, combined with a complex verbal and linguistic pattern in depth." (Robert Martin Adams, *Milton and the Modern Critics*, Ithaca, Cornell University Press, 1955, p.198) Milton's poetry is simply too large, and too densely packed, to be dealt with adequately only on the prosodic level.

d. had WE/ but WORLD/ eNOUGH,/ and TIME,/
     this COY/ness, LA/dy, WERE/ no CRIME./
     WE would/ sit DOWN,/ and THINK/ which WAY/
     to WALK,/ and PASS/ our LONG/ love's DAY./
     THOU by/ the IN/dian GAN/ges SIDE/   5
     should'st RU/bies FIND;/ I by/ the TIDE/
     of HUM/ber WOULD/ comPLAIN./ I would/
     LOVE you/ ten YEARS/ beFORE/ the FLOOD,/
     and YOU/ should, IF/ you PLEASE/ reFUSE/
     TILL the/ conVER/sion OF/ the JEWS./   10
     my VE/geTA/ble LOVE/ should GROW/
     VASter/ than EM/pires, AND/ more SLOW./
     an HUN/dred YEARS/ should GO/ to PRAISE/
     thine EYES,/ and ON/ thy FORE/head GAZE./
     two HUN/dred TO/ aDORE/ each BREAST,/   15
     but THIR/ty THOU/sand TO/ the REST;/
     an AGE/ at LEAST/ to EVE/ry PART,/
     AND the/LAST age/ should SHOW/ your HEART./
     for LA/dy YOU/ deSERVE/ this STATE,/
     nor WOULD/ i LOVE/ at LO/wer RATE./   20
          but AT/ my BACK/ i AL/ways HEAR/
     time's WIN/ged CHA/rriot HUR/rying NEAR:/
     and YON/der ALL/ beFORE/ us LYE/
     DEsarts/ of VAST/ eTER/niTY./
     thy BEAU/ty SHALL/ no MORE/ be FOUND,/   25
     NOR in/ thy MAR/ble VAULT/ shall SOUND/
     my ECH/oing SONG;/ then WORMS/ shall TRY/
     that LONG/ preSERV'D/ virGI/niTY,/
     and YOUR/ quaint HO/nour TURN/ to DUST,/
     and IN/to A/shes ALL/ my LUST./   30
     the GRAVE'S/ a FINE/ and PRI/vate PLACE,/
     but NONE/ i THINK/ do THERE/ embRACE./
          now THERE/fore, WHILE/ the YOUTH/ful HEW/
     SITS on/ thy SKIN/ like MOR/ning DEW,/
     and WHILE/ thy WILL/ing SOUL/ tranSPIRES/   35
     at EVE/ry PORE/ with IN/stant FIRES,/
     now LET/ us SPORT/ us WHILE/ we MAY,/
     and NOW,/ like AM/'rous BIRDS/ of PREY/
     RAther/ at ONCE/ our TIME/ deVOUR/
     than LAN/guish IN/ his SLOW/-chapt POW'R./   40

LET us/ roll ALL/ our STRENGTH,/ and ALL/
our SWEET/ness, UP/ inTO/ one BALL,/
and TEAR/ our PLEA/sures WITH/ rough STRIFE/
thoROUGH/ the IR/on GATES/ of LIFE./
THUS, though/ we CAN/not MAKE/ our SUN/   45
stand STILL,/ yet WE/ will MAKE/ him RUN./
            (Andrew Marvell, "To his Coy Mistress,"
                              mid–17th cent.?)

Marvell's fondness for reversed feet may have influenced my scansion of line seven: since "would" is the rhyme-word for "flood" it would ordinarily be given metrical stress—and perhaps should have that stress here. The same reasoning lies behind my scansion of the first foot of line forty-five, which could almost as well be reversed. Line eighteen shows us Marvell sprinting into a genuine trochaic measure—but only for two metrical feet, after which he returns to the basic iambic. This is a variant that, over time, grows increasingly more common.

e.   i SAW/ eTER/niTY/ the O/ther NIGHT/
       LIKE a/ great RING/ of PURE/ and END/less LIGHT,/
             all CALM,/ as IT/ was BRIGHT,/
       and ROUND/ beNEATH/ it, TIME/ in HOURS,/
             days, YEARS/
                 DRIV'N by/ the SPHERES/   5
       LIKE a/ vast SHA/dow MOV'D,/ in WHICH/ the
             WORLD/
         and ALL/ her TRAIN/ were HURL'D./
       the DO/ting LO/ver IN/ his QUEIN/test
             STRAIN/
                did THEIR/ comPLAIN,/
       NEER him,/ his LUTE,/ his FAN/cy, AND/ his
             FLIGHTS,/   10
              wit's SOUR/ deLIGHTS,/
       with GLOVES,/ and KNOTS/ the SIL/ly SNARES/
             of PLEAsure,/
              yet HIS/ dear TREAsure/
       all SCAT/ter'd LAY,/ while HE/ his EYS/ did POUR/
             upON/ a FLOWR./   15
       (Henry Vaughan, "The World," 1650: excerpt)

72

f. THEY are/ all GONE/ INto/ the WORLD/ of LIGHT!/
     and I/ aLONE/ sit LIN/gring HERE;/
    their VE/ry ME/moRY/ is FAIR/ and BRIGHT,/
           and MY/ sad THOUGHTS/ doth CLEAR./

    it GLOWS/ and GLIT/ters IN/ my CLOU/dy BREST/   5
     like STARS/ upON/ some GLOO/my GROVE,/
    or THOSE/ faint BEAMS/ in WHICH/ this HILL/ is
      DREST/
          AFter/ the SUN'S/ reMOVE./

    i SEE/ them WAL/king IN/ an AIR/ of GLOry,/
     whose LIGHT/ doth TRAM/ple ON/ my DAYS:/   10
    my DAYS,/ which ARE/ at BEST/ but DULL/ and
      HOAry,/
          meer GLI/mering AND/ deCAYS./

    o HO/ly HOPE!/ and HIGH/ huMI/liTY,/
     HIGH as/ the HEA/vens aBOVE!/
    THESE are/ your WALKS,/ and YOU/ have SHEW'D/
      them ME/   15
          to KIN/dle MY/ cold LOVE./

    dear, BEAU/teous DEATH!/ the JE/wel OF/ the JUST,/
     SHIning/ no WHERE,/ but IN/ the DARK;/
    what MY/steRIES/ do LIE/ beYOND/ thy DUST,/
          could MAN/ outLOOK/ that MARK!/   20

    HE that/ hath FOUND/ some FLEDG'D/ bird's
     NEST/ may KNOW/
    at FIRST/ SIGHT if/ the BIRD/ be FLOWN;/
    but WHAT/ fair WELL/ or GROVE/ he SINGS/ in NOW,/
     THAT is, to HIM/ unKNOWN./
          (Henry Vaughan, "They Are All Gone into the
          World of Light," 1655: excerpt)

12 / Dryden, Swift,
Prior, and Pope

a. ah FAD/ing JOY,/ how QUICK/ly ART/ thou PAST?/
            yet WE/ thy RU/ine HASTE:/
     as IF/ the CARES/ of HU/mane LIFE/ were FEW/
              we SEEK/ out NEW:/
     and FOL/low FATE/ which WOULD/ too FAST/ purSUE./   5

     see HOW/ on EVE/ry BOUGH/ the BIRDS/ exPRESS/
         in THEIR/ sweet NOTES/ their HAP/piNESS./
     they ALL/ enJOY,/ and NO/thing SPARE;/
     but ON/ their MO/ther NA/ture LAY/ their CARE:/
     why THEN/ should MAN,/ the LORD/ of ALL/ beLOW,/   10
         such TROU/bles CHUSE/ to KNOW/
     as NONE/ of ALL/ his SUB/jects UN/derGO?/

     hark, HARK,/ the WA/ters FALL,/ fall, FALL;/
     and WITH/ a MUR/muring SOUND/
     dash, DASH,/ upON/ the GROUND,/   15
         to GEN/tle SLUM/bers CALL./
     (John Dryden, "Song," from *The Indian Emperor*, 1665)

The one metrical irregularity, the possibly trisyllabic foot in line
fourteen, may not be irregular at all, since in Dryden's time (as
today) British English often reduces words like "murmuring" to
two syllables. Dryden skillfully avoids the mechanical beat of
poems like Joyce Kilmer's relentlessly regular "Trees" by varying line-length, stanza-length, and rhyme-pattern. Still, the com-

paratively icy smoothness of too much Augustan poetry has clearly settled down. Dryden's "song" is remarkably unmusical for so deft and craftsmanlike a piece, nor does it carry any significant quantity of emotion (public or personal) or thought. The reader/listener is directed, not challenged; he is soothed, not enlightened. And the prosody is one of the tools by which this is accomplished.

b.   as WHEN/ a TREE'S/ cut DOWN/ the SE/cret ROOT/
       lives UN/derGROUND,/ and THENCE/ new
          BRAN/ches SHOOT;/
       so FROM/ old SHAKE/spear's HO/nour'd DUST,/ this
          DAY/
       springs UP/ and BUDS/ a NEW/ reVI/ving PLAY:/
       SHAKEspear,/ who (TAUGHT/ by NONE)/ did FIRST/
          imPART/   5
       to FLET/cher WIT,/ to LA/bouring* JON/son ART./
       he MO/narch-LIKE/ gave THOSE/ his SUB/jects LAW,/
       and IS/ that NA/ture WHICH/ they PAINT/ and DRAW./
       FLETcher/ reach'd THAT/ which ON/ his HEIGHTS/
          did GROW,/
       whilst JON/son CREPT/ and GA/ther'd ALL/
          beLOW./   10
       THIS† did/ his LOVE,/ and THIS‡/ his MIRTH/
          diGEST:/
       one I/miTATES/ him MOST,/ the O/ther BEST./
       if THEY/ have SINCE/ out-WRIT/ all O/ther MEN,/
       'tis WITH/ the DROPS/ which FELL/ from
          SHAKE/spear's PEN./
            (Dryden, "Prologue" to *The Tempest*, 1670: excerpt)

    *-ouring = monosyllabic
    †i.e., Fletcher
    ‡i.e., Jonson

This is regular not only in prosody but in form: Dryden keeps the so-called "heroic couplet" (iambic pentameter, end-stopped, rhyming) from rhythmic stasis by deft placement of the caesura (sometimes strong, sometimes weak), which usually occurs after the second or third foot. The pattern here, line by line, is caesura after:

line 1	3rd foot
line 2	2nd foot
line 3	4th foot
line 4	2nd foot
line 5	1st and 3rd feet
line 6	2nd foot
line 7	2nd foot
line 8	2nd foot
line 9	2nd foot
line 10	mid–4th foot
line 11	2nd foot
line 12	3rd foot
line 13	3rd foot
line 14	3rd foot

Dryden exploits these possibilities well; as we will see, Pope, the consummate master of the heroic couplet, exploits them still better. Dryden's ear is sure, but Pope's is delicate.

c.   all HU/mane THINGS/ are SUB/ject TO/ deCAY,/
     and, WHEN/ fate SUM/mons, MO/narchs MUST/
        oBEY:/
     this FLEC/kno FOUND,/ who, LIKE/ auGUS/tus,
        YOUNG/
     was CALL'D/ to EM/pire, AND/ had GO/vern'd LONG;/
     in PROSE/ and VERSE,/ was OWN'D,/ withOUT/
        disPUTE,/   5
     through ALL/ the REALMS/ of NON/-sense,
        AB/soLUTE./
     this A/ged PRINCE/ now FLOU/riSHING/ in PEACE,/
     and BLEST/ with IS/sue OF/ a LARGE/ inCREASE,/
     worn OUT/ with BUSI/ness*, DID/ at LENGTH/
        deBATE/
     to SET/tle THE/ sucCES/sion OF/ the STATE;/   10
     and POND/'ring WHICH/ of ALL/ his SONS/ was FIT/
     to REIGN,/ and WAGE/ imMOR/tal WAR/ with WIT,/
     cry'd, 'TIS/ reSOLV'D;/ for NA/ture PLEADS/ that HE/
     should ONE/ly RULE,/ who MOST/ reSEM/bles ME./
                          (Dryden, "Mac Flecknoe," 1679: excerpt)

---
*bisyllabic, as today

76

Satiric rather than serious verse calls for different prosodic patterns, and Dryden supplies them. The caesura (sometimes, indeed, barely more than what musicians might call a "rest") occurs, here, line by line, after:

line 1	2nd foot
line 2	2nd foot
line 3	2nd and 4th feet
line 4	2nd foot
line 5	2nd and 3rd feet
line 6	4th foot
line 7	2nd foot
line 8	2nd foot
line 9	2nd foot
line 10	3rd foot
line 11	mid–2nd foot
line 12	1st foot
line 13	2nd foot
line 14	2nd foot

d. . . . now FROM/ all PARTS/ the SWEL/ling
        KEN/nels* FLOW,/
    and BEAR/ their TRO/phies WITH/ them AS/ they GO:/
    FILTH of/ all HUES/ and O/dours SEEM/ to TELL/
    what STREETS/ they SAIL'D/ from, BY/ the
        SIGHT and SMELL./
    THEY, as/ each TOR/rent DRIVES,/ with RA/pid
        FORCE,/   5
    from SMITH/field OR/ saint PUL/chre's SHAPE/
        their COURSE,/
    and IN/ huge CON/fluent† JOIN/ at SNOW/-hill
        RIDGE,/
    FALL from/ the CON/duit† PRONE/ to HOL/born-
        BRIDGE./
    SWEEPings/ from BUT/chers' STALLS,/ dung,
        GUTS,/ and BLOOD,/
    drown'd PUP/pies, STINK/ing SPRATS‡,/ all
        DRENCH'D/ in MUD,/   10

77

dead CATS/ and TUR/nip-TOPS/ come TUM/bling
DOWN/ the FLOOD./
(Jonathan Swift, ''A Description of a
City Shower,'' 1710:
excerpt)

---

*kennels = gutters
†bisyllabic
‡sprats = herring

The triplet which ends both this excerpt and the poem features a
final line in iambic hexameter. Note that Swift varies the prosody
more than does Dryden: for example, four of the eleven lines
here quoted begin with reverse iambic feet (though the first foot
of line eight may well be meant to be scanned as regular iambic).

e. inTERR'D/ beNEATH/ this MAR/ble STONE/
    lie SAUNT/'ring JACK,/ and I/dle JOAN./
    while ROL/ling THREE/score YEARS/ and ONE/
    did ROUND/ this WORLD/ their COUR/ses RUN,/
    if HU/man THINGS/ went ILL/ or WELL,/   5
    if CHAN/ging EM/pires ROSE/ or FELL,/
    the MOR/ning PAST,/ the EVE/ning CAME,/
    and FOUND/ this COU/ple STILL/ the SAME./
    they WALK'D/ and EAT*,/ good FOLKS:/ what THEN?/
    why THEN/ they WALK'D/ and EAT*/ aGAIN./   10
    they SOUND/ly SLEPT/ the NIGHT/ aWAY;/
    they DID/ just NO/thing ALL/ the DAY;/
    and HA/ving BU/ry'd CHIL/dren FOUR,/
    wou'd NOT/ take PAINS/ to TRY/ for MORE./
Matthew Prior, ''An Epitaph,'' 1718: excerpt)

---

*pronounced ''et''

Using a tetrameter rather than the pentameter couplet, Prior is
obliged to handle the caesura very differently. Many lines have
no caesura at all (lines one, three, four, five, six, eleven, thirteen).
And even though the even number of feet makes a caesura after
foot two seem more symmetrical than satisfying, Prior produces
considerable variety, interspersing swifter, uninterrupted lines
with more slowly cadenced ones. In line nine, indeed, he manages

not one but two pronounced pauses, thus producing still greater prosodic variation. In lines fifty-seven and sixty-one, not quoted above, he in fact employs a caesura after each foot: the poem's final lines are a veritable burst of prosodic fireworks:

nor GOOD,/ nor BAD,/ nor FOOLS,/ nor WISE;/
they WOU'D/ not LEARN,/ nor COU'D/ adVISE:/
withOUT/ love, HA/tred, JOY,/ or FEAR,/
they LED/—a KIND/ of—AS/ it WERE:/   60
nor WISH'D,/ nor CAR'D,/ nor LAUGH'D,/ nor
   CRY'D:/
and SO/ they LIV'D;/ and SO/ they DY'D./

f.   what DIRE/ ofFENCE/ from AM/'rous CAU/ses
       SPRINGS,/
    what MIGH/ty CON/tests RISE/ from TRI/vial*
       THINGS,/
    i SING/—this VERSE/ to CA/ryll, MUSE,/ is DUE;/
    this, EV'N/ beLIN/da MAY/ vouchSAFE/ to VIEW:/
    SLIGHT is/ the SUB/ject, BUT/ not SO/ the PRAISE,/   5
    if SHE/ inSPIRE, and HE/ apPROVE/ my LAYS./
       say WHAT/ strange MO/tive, GOD/dess! COU'D/
       comPEL/
    a WELL/-bred LORD/ t'asSAULT/ a GEN/tle BELLE?/
    oh SAY/ what STRAN/ger CAUSE,/ yet UN/exPLOR'D,/
    coul'd MAKE/ a GEN/tle BELLE/ reJECT/ a LORD?/   10
    in TASKS/ so BOLD,/ can LIT/tle MEN/ enGAGE,/
    and IN/ soft BO/soms DWELLS/ such MIGH/ty RAGE?/
       (Alexander Pope, "The Rape of the Lock," 1714: excerpt)

*bisyllabic

g.   say FIRST,/ of GOD/ aBOVE,/ or MAN/ beLOW,/
    WHAT can/ we REA/son, BUT/ from WHAT/ we
       KNOW?/
    of MAN/ what SEE/ we, BUT/ his STA/tion HERE,/
    from WHICH/ to REA/son, OR/ to WHICH/ reFER?/
    thro' WORLDS/ unNUM/ber'd THO'/ the GOD/ be
       KNOWN,/   5
    'tis OURS/ to TRACE/ him ON/ly IN/ our OWN./

he, WHO/ thro VAST/ imMEN/siTY/ can PIERCE,/
see WORLDS/ on WORLDS/ comPOSE/ one
    U/niVERSE,/
obSERVE/ how SYS/tem IN/to SYS/tem RUNS,/
what O/ther PLA/nets CIR/cle O/ther SUNS,/   10
what VA/ry'd BE/ing PEO/ples EV/'ry STAR,/
may TELL/ why HEAV'N/ has MADE/ us AS/ we ARE./
BUT of/ this FRAME/ the BEA/rings, AND/ the TIES,/
the STRONG, conNEC/tions, NICE/ dePEN/denCIES,/
graDA/tions JUST,/ has THY/ perVA/ding SOUL/   15
look'd THRO'?/ or CAN/ a PART/ conTAIN/ the
    WHOLE?/

        (Pope, "An Essay On Man," Epistle I, 1733: excerpt)

Pope's placement of the caesura is nothing short of amazingly
varied. Line by line in this passage, the caesura comes after:

line 1	1st and 3rd feet
line 2	2nd foot
line 3	mid 3rd foot
line 4	mid 3rd foot
line 5	2nd foot
line 6	2nd foot
line 7	mid 1st foot
line 8	2nd foot
line 9	mid 3rd foot
line 10	mid 3rd foot
line 11	mid 3rd foot
line 12	2nd foot
line 13	mid 4th foot
line 14	mid 3rd foot
line 15	2nd foot
line 16	1st foot

In these matters, Pope is a bit like composers who find the
ordinary half-tone scales too coarse, and rely instead on quarter-
tones, or even finer gradations.

h.   shut, SHUT/ the DOOR,/ good JOHN!/ faTIGU'D,/ i
        SAID,/
tye UP/ the KNOC/ker, SAY/ i'm SICK, i'm DEAD./
the DOG/-star RA/ges! NAY/ 'tis PAST/ a DOUBT/
all BED/lam, OR/ parNAS/sus IS/ let OUT:/
FIRE in/ each EYE,/ and PA/pers IN/ each HAND,/   5
they RAVE,/ reCITE,/ and MAD/den ROUND/ the
        LAND./
     what WALLS/ can GUARD/ me, OR/ what
        SHADES/ can HIDE?/
they PIERCE/ my THIC/kets, THRO'/ my GROT/ they
        GLIDE,/
by LAND,/ by WA/ter, THEY/ reNEW/ the CHARGE,/
they STOP/ the CHA/riot* AND/ they BOARD/ the
        BARGE./   10
no PLACE/ is SA/cred, NOT/ the CHURCH/ is FREE,/
ev'n SUN/day SHINES/ no SAB/bath-DAY/ to ME:/
then FROM/ the MINT/ walks FORTH/ the MAN/ of
        RHYME,/
HAPpy!/ to CATCH/ me, JUST/ at DIN/ner-TIME./
     IS there/ a PAR/son, MUCH/ be-MUS'D/ in
        BEER,/   15
a MAU/dlin PO/eTESS,/ a RHY/ming PEER,/
a CLERK,/ foreDOOM'D/ his FA/ther's SOUL/ to
        CROSS,/
who PENS/ a STAN/za WHEN/ he SHOULD/
        enGROSS?†/
IS there,/ who LOCK'D/ from INK/ and PA/per,
        SCRAWLS/
with DESP/'rate CHAR/coal ROUND/ his DAR/ken'd
        WALLS?/   20
all FLY/ to TWIT/'nam, AND/ in HUM/ble STRAIN,/
apPLY/ to ME,/ to KEEP/ them MAD/ or VAIN./
ARthur/ whose GID/dy SON/ neGLECTS/ the LAWS,/
imPUTES/ to ME/ and MY/ damn'd WORKS/ the
        CAUSE./
poor COR/nus SEES/ his FRAN/tic WIFE/ eLOPE,/   25
and CUR/ses WIT,/ and PO/eTRY, and POPE./
       (Pope, "Epistle to Dr. Arbuthnot," 1735: excerpt)

---

*bisyllabic
†engross = to compile; to write legal documents

Pope fashions his verse, here, with such supple, free-flowing movement, that even using the comparatively rigid heroic couplet he manages to re-create the rhythms of colloquial speech. It is a prosodic achievement beyond praise; it is also inimitable.

13 / Smart, Cowper, and Blake

a.   o THOU,/ that SIT'ST/ upON/ a THRONE,/
           with HARP/ of HIGH/ maJES/tic TONE,/
               to PRAISE/ the KING/ of KINGS;/
           and VOICE/ of HEAV'N/-aSCEND/ing SWELL,/
           which, WHILE/ its DEE/per NOTES/ exCEL,/   5
               CLEAR, as/ a CLA/rion*, RINGS:/

           to BLESS/ each VAL/ley, GROVE/ and COAST,/
           and CHARM/ the CHE/rubs TO/ the POST/
               of GRA/tiTUDE/ in THRONGS;/
           to KEEP/ the DAYS/ on ZI/on's MOUNT,/   10
           and SEND/ the YEAR/ to HIS/ acCOUNT,/
           with DAN/ces AND/ with SONGS./
               (Christopher Smart, "A Song to David," 1763:
                                       excerpt)

*bisyllabic

Although Smart was without question mentally unstable, and this poem is said to have been written on the walls of a mental institution, the prosody is unexceptionable. The same is true of the poetry written during his more or less stable periods:

b.   NOW'S/ the TIME/ for MIRTH/ and PLAY,/
           SA/turDAY'S/ an HO/liDAY;/
           PRAISE/ to HEAV'N/ unCEA/sing YIELD,/
           i've FOUND/ a LARK'S/ nest IN/ the FIELD./

a LARK'S/ nest, THEN/ your PLAY/mate BEGS/   5
you'd SPARE/ herSELF/ and SPEC/kled EGGS;/
SOON/ she SHALL/ aSCEND/ and SING/
your PRAI/ses TO/ th'eTER/nal KING./
(Smart, "Hymn XXXIII," 1770)

Not only does Smart make careful, appropriate use of the prosodic apostrophe, here, he is keenly aware of the realities of the
English language. The stress pattern on compounds like "lark's
nest" is invariably high on the first word and low on the second,
thus permitting Smart to not once but twice use the second word,
"nest," as the metrically unstressed syllable in a poetic foot.
Whatever signs of Smart's problems this little poem may reflect,
they do not seem to affect the prosody.

c.   *For I will consider my Cat Jeoffry.*
    For he is the servant of the Living God duly and daily
             serving him.
    For at the first glance of the glory of God in the East he
             worships in his way.
    For is this done by wreathing his body seven times
             round with elegant quickness.
    For then he leaps up to catch the musk, which is the
             blessing of God upon his prayer.   5
    For he rolls upon prank to work it in.
    For having done duty and received blessing he begins
             to consider himself.
    For this he performs in ten degrees.
    For first he looks upon his fore-paws to see if they are
             clean.
    For secondly he kicks up behind to clear away there.   10
    For thirdly he works it upon stretch with the fore paws
             extended.
    For fourthly he sharpens his paws by wood.
    For fifthly he washes himself.
    For sixthly he rolls upon wash.
    For seventhly he fleas himself, that he may not be
             interrupted upon the beat.   15
    For eighthly he rubs himself against a post.
    For ninthly he looks up for his instructions.

For tenthly he goes in quest of food.
For having considered God and himself he will consider
      his neighbor.   20
For if he meets another cat he will kiss her in kindness.
For when he takes his prey he plays with it to give it a
      chance.
For one mouse in seven escapes by his dallying.
For when his day's work is done his business more
      properly begins.
For he keeps the Lord's watch in the night against the
      adversary.   25
For he counteracts the powers of darkness by his
      electrical skin and glaring eyes.
For he counteracts the Devil, who is death, by brisking
      about the life.
For in his morning orisons he loves the sun and the sun
      loves him.
For he is of the tribe of Tiger. . . .
            (Smart, "Jubilate Agno," 1756–63: excerpt)

The signs of madness are all over this poem, to be sure. But it is far too easy to attribute each and all the component parts, and especially those having to do with prosody and other technical matters, simply and exclusively to mental instability. As we have seen, Smart's prosody, whether written during sane or insane times, is not only indistinguishable from the prosody of more normal poets but, more to the point here, is also indistinguishable one from the other. Sane or insane, he is, like most artists, capable of handling technical matters with trained ease. We need only think of Robert Schumann, some of whose most exciting (and substantively unusual) compositions were written during mad periods, or Vincent Van Gogh, many if not most of whose paintings were produced while the artist's mind was seriously disturbed. It is of course possible that Smart's illness was different, from one insane period to another. But this is unlikely to have caused so significant and startling a technical difference: artists whose mental problems interfere with their technique usually show either sharply diminished technical facility or else simply stop practicing their art.

And there is a good deal more to consider, too. The tighter

and more restrictive become an art's bonds, the more likely becomes some explosive counter-thrust. This is too obvious and well-documented a truism to need discussion; the work of William Blake, to be considered shortly, plainly fits that bill very well, as a century later so does the work of Gerard Manley Hopkins. The doldrum state of late Victorian English poetry, on both sides of the Atlantic, is pretty universally conceded. And not only does Smart anticipate Blake's use of biblically-derived, half chant-like rhythms, but he also plainly anticipates both the same development in the work of Walt Whitman, as well as Whitman's fondness for end-stopped lines (no matter what their length) and "laundry lists." (There are interesting rhetorical similarities, as well, but those fall outside the scope of this book.)

And there are other mad poets to consider, finally, notably William Cowper, who was only nine years Smart's junior.

d.   i SING/ the SO/fa, I,/ who LATE/ly SANG/
     truth, HOPE,/ and CHA/riTY,/ and TOUCHED/ with
          AWE/
     the SO/lemn CHORDS,/ and WITH/ a TREM/bling
          HAND,/
     esCAPED/ with PAIN/ from THAT/ adVEN/t'rous
          FLIGHT,/
     now SEEK/ rePOSE/ upON/ an HUM/bler THEME;/   5
     the THEME/ though HUM/ble, YET/ auGUST,/ and
          PROUD/
     th'ocCA/sion—FOR/ the FAIR/ comMANDS/ the
          SONG./
          time WAS,/ when CLO/thing SUMP/tuous OR/ for
          USE,/
     save THEIR/ own PAIN/ted SKINS,/ our SIRES/ had
          NONE./
     as YET/ black BREE/ches WERE/ not; SA/tin
          SMOOTH,/   10
     or VEL/vet SOFT,/ or PLUSH/ with SHAG/gy PILE;/
     the HAR/dy CHIEF/ upON/ the RUG/ged ROCK/
     WASHED by/ the SEA,/ or ON/ the GRA/velly BANK/
     thrown UP/ by WIN/try TOR/rents ROA/ring LOUD,/
     FEARless/ of WRONG,/ rePOSED/ his WEA/ry
          STRENGTH./   15

those BAR/'brous A/ges PAST,/ sucCEED/ed NEXT/
the BIRTH/-day OF/ inVEN/tion; WEAK/ at FIRST,/
DULL in/ deSIGN,/ and CLUM/sy TO/ perFORM./
JOINT-stools/ were THEN/ creA/ted; ON/ three LEGS/
upBORNE/ they STOOD./ . . .   20

    (William Cowper, "The Task," 1785: excerpt)

e.   OH! for/ a CLO/ser WALK/ with GOD,/
          a CALM/ and HEAV'N/ly FRAME;/
          a LIGHT/ to SHINE/ upON/ the ROAD/
          that LEADS/ me TO/ the LAMB!/

          WHERE is/ the BLES/sedNESS/ i KNEW/   5
          when FIRST/ i SAW/ the LORD?/
          WHERE is/ the SOUL/-reFRE/shing VIEW/
          of JE/sus, AND/ his WORD?/

          what PEACE/ful HOURS/ i ONCE/ enJOYED!/
          how SWEET/ their MEM/'ry STILL!/   10
          but THEY/ have LEFT/ an ACH/ing VOID/
          the WORLD/ can NE/ver FILL./
          (Cowper, "Olney Hymns," I, 1771–72: excerpt)

Although Cowper was frequently insane, and died so, his
prosody is clearly unexceptionable—and as the next poem dem-
onstrates, was equally unexceptionable in either state.

f.   HA/tred/ and VEN/geance, MY/ eTER/nal PORtion,/
     SCARCE can/ enDURE/ deLAY/ of EX/eCUtion,/
     WAIT, with/ imPA/tient REA/diNESS,/ to SEIZE my/
          SOUL in/ a MOment./

     DAMNED be/low JU/das: MORE/ abHORRED/ than
          HE was,/   5
     WHO for/ a FEW/ pence SOLD/ his HO/ly MASter./
     TWICE be/tray'd JE/sus ME,/ the LAST/ deLINquent,/
          DEEMS the/proFAnest./

     MAN dis/aVOWS,/ and DE/iTY/ disOWNS me:/
     HELL might/ afFORD/ my MI/seRIES/ a SHELter;/   10

THEREfore/ hell KEEPS/ her E/ver HUN/gry MOUTHS
    all/
BOLted/ aGAINST me./

HARD lot!/ enCOM/passed WITH/ a THOU/sand
    DANgers;/
WEAry,/ faint, TREM/bling WITH/ a THOU/sand
    TERrors;/
I'M called,/ if VAN/quished, TO/ reCEIVE/ a SENtence/   15
    WORSE than/ aBIram's./

HIM the/ vinDIC/tive ROD/ of AN/gry JUStice/
SENT quick/ and HOW/ling TO/ the CEN/ter
    HEADlong;/
I, fed/ with JUDG/ment, IN/ a FLE/shly TOMB, am/
    BUried/ aBOVE ground./
  (Cowper, "Lines Written During a Period of Insanity," 1774)

This baroquely elaborate little poem strongly corroborates the assertion, above, that prosodic technique is not apt to be affected by mere insanity. Indeed, what Cowper thought he was doing, here, was metrically even more elaborate than might appear, because his intent was to imitate, in English, the Sapphic metric, a complex Aeolic pattern copied by Latin and later by many European literatures. It would not be hard to imagine many saner folk succeeding nowhere near so well, under such limiting circumstances, with the demands of a basically iambic pentameter meter, the first foot consistently reversed, the last foot consistently ending in a feminine syllable, and in a four-line stanza-form regularly setting three lines of this meter against a concluding iambic dimeter line in the same strict pattern, an initial reversed foot and a final feminine syllable.

g.   "i HAVE/ no NAME:/
                   i AM/ but TWO/ days OLD."/
                   WHAT shall/ i CALL thee?/
                   "i HAP/py AM,/
                   JOY is/ my NAME."/
                   sweet JOY/ beFALL thee!/   5

PRET/ty JOY!/
sweet JOY/ but TWO/ days OLD,/
sweet JOY/ i CALL thee:/
THOU/ dost SMILE,/   10
i SING/ the WHILE,/
sweet JOY/ beFALL thee!/
(William Blake, "Infant Joy," 1789)

h.   how SWEET/ is the SHEP/herd's sweet LOT!/
from the MORN/ to the EVE/ning he STRAYS;/
he shall FOL/low his SHEEP/ all the DAY,/
and his TONGUE/ shall be FILLED/ with PRAISE./

for he HEARS/ the LAMB'S/ INno/cent CALL,/   5
and he HEARS/ the EWE'S/ TENder/ rePLY;/
he is WATCH/ful WHILE/ they ARE/ in PEACE,/
for they KNOW/ when their SHEP/herd is NIGH./
(Blake, "The Shepherd," 1789)

As these two poems from *Songs of Innocence* show, Blake's
early prosody is sometimes fairly standard, and sometimes shows
high order irregularities. The first thing to happen, when the
Chaucerian Compromise begins to come apart, is—inevitably—a
loosening of the foreign, syllable-counting element. "Infant Joy"
can be viewed either as a continuation of standard traditional
prosody or, because it is eccentrically traditional, a harbinger of
things to come. But "The Shepherd" clearly shows a loosening
of the syllable-counting element: of the twelve metrical feet in
the first stanza, ten are trisyllablic, and there are six more
trisyllablic feet in the second stanza—which is distinctly eccentric, since for the trimeter of stanza one it substitutes three lines
of tetrameter and a final line of trimeter.

i.   o ROSE,/ thou art SICK!/
the inVI/sible WORM/
that FLIES/ in the NIGHT,/
in the HOW/ling STORM,/

has FOUND/ out thy BED/   5
of CRIM/son JOY:/

and his DARK/ secret LOVE/
does thy LIFE/ desTROY./
(Blake, "The Sick Rose," 1794)

j.   AH,/ SUN-flower!/ WEAry/ of TIME,/
who COUN/test the STEPS/ of the SUN,/
SEEking/ AFter/ that SWEET/ golden CLIME/
where the TRA/veller's JOUR/ney is DONE;/

where the YOUTH/ pined aWAY/ with deSIRE,/   5
and the pale VIR/gin SHROU/ded in SNOW/
aRISE/ from their GRAVES,/ and asPIRE/
where my SUN/-flower WI/shes to GO./
(Blake, "Ah! Sun-Flower," 1794)

Just a few years later, these two poems from *Songs of Experience* show markedly larger and more significant prosodic irregularities. "The Sick Rose," for which Blake has chosen a nominally dimeter meter, has sixteen metrical feet, of which more than 50%—nine—are trisyllabic. Such a high percentage of irregular feet comes close to destroying the sense that the poem is built on any underlining metrical pattern other than the requirement of two stresses per line. How sensibly can we talk of either a basic iambic dimeter metric, or an anapestic dimeter metric, when the poem contains about half of one and half of the other, mixed (or one might better say jumbled) together according to no observable pattern? This is clearly a victory for the nativist or stress-related side of the Chaucerian Compromise, and a defeat for the foreign or syllable-counting side.

The second poem, "Ah! Sun-Flower," is metrically so jumbled that no semblance of stanzaically replicative metrics is left. The first stanza, though it does not follow standard patterns (I will say more of this in a moment), is at least in a 4-3-4-3 mold of some sort. The second stanza, however, is either 3-3-3-3, as here scanned, or 3-4-3-3, if line six is marked "AND the/ pale VIR/gin SHROUD/ed in SNOW/." But how does one decide which scansion of the line best fits the overall pattern, when the overall pattern barely seems to exist? The first line encapsulates the difficulty: should it be scanned as it is here, or is there to be a severe wrenching about of the word "SUN-flower," in order to oblige line one (and also line eight) to fit a more traditional metrical pattern, namely, "AH, sun/-FLOWer!/ WEAry/ of TIME," and, for line eight, "WHERE my/ sun-FLOW/er WI/ shes to GO./" But not only is this wrenching about alien to the obvious spirit of Blake's poem, and of everything we know about Blake and his thinking, we also have the counter-evidence of the title. It is not conclusive evidence, but it is fairly persuasive, that Blake has in the title put an exclamation mark rather than a comma (as in the text of the poem) after the word "Ah," thus making it difficult not to prolong that word and virtually impossible to avoid the natural linguistic stress on the first word of the compound "sun-flower." And in this second poem, too, of a total of (as here scanned) twenty-six metrical feet, sixteen are trisyllabic, one is monosyllabic, and line six (again, as here scanned) has four syllables. Even the possible revisions of lines one and eight, just discussed, would only reduce the total of metrically irregular feet to just over 50%. And that still does not take into the further irregularity of line three, which opens with what can only be described as a brace of trochaic feet.

k.   i ASK/ed* a THIEF/ to STEAL/ me a PEACH:/
      he TURNED/ up his EYES./
      i ASK'D/ a lithe LA/dy to LIE/ her DOWN:/
      HOly/ and MEEK/ she CRIES —/

      as SOON/ as i WENT/
      an AN/gel CAME./
      he WINK'D/ at the THIEF/
      and SMIL'D/ at the DAME./

      and withOUT/ one word SAID/
      had a PEACH/ from the TREE/
      and STILL/ as a MAID/
      enJOY'D/ the laDY./
                    (Blake, "I Asked a Thief," 1796)
      _____
      *bisyllabic, as marked by Blake

Blake has clearly not thrown off the Chaucerian Compromise, here. The carefully marked distinction between "asked" and

10

"ask'd," as well as the traditional though awkward scansion of "laDY," to ensure a proper rhyme, plainly indicate Chaucerian-Compromise notions. On the other hand, it has become essentially impossible to say either what metric or what metrical pattern the poem is written in. Not only do iambs and anapests mingle so freely and loosely that it is hard to justify calling them iambs and anapests at all, but line lengths vary according to no known principle. (Line nine may well be scanned "AND with/ OUT one/ word SAID/": it is impossible to know for sure.)

1.   to SEE/ a WORLD/ in a GRAIN/ of SAND/
       and a HEA/ven in a *wild flower*,
       HOLD in/FInity/ in the PALM/ of your HAND/
       and eTER/nity IN/ an HOur*./

       a RO/bin RED/ breast IN/ a CAGE/   5
       PUTS/ all HEA/ven IN/ a RAGE./
       a DOVE/ house FILL'D/ with DOVES/ and PIgeons/
       SHUD/ders HELL/ thro' ALL/ its REgions./
       a DOG/ STARV'D at/ his MAS/ter's GATE/
       preDICTS/ the RU/in OF/ the STATE./ . . .   10
          (Blake, "Auguries of Innocence," 1803?: excerpt)

*bisyllabic, to rhyme with FLOWer?

Still Chaucerian-Compromise verse, this one hundred and thirty-two-line poem is close to doggerel. Throughout most of its length, it varies unpredictably between three and four feet per line, and the feet vary from monosyllabic to trisyllabic, according to no obvious principle. Line two, indeed, is almost impossible to scan authoritatively: it could be anything from iambic pentameter ("AND/ a HEA/ven IN/ a WI/ld FLOWer/"—where "wild is, like "RUin" in line ten, bisyllabic) to trimeter ("and a HEA/ven in a WILD/ FLOWer/"). But how are we to know? Plainly, though Blake still employs what at least look like prosodic apostrophe markings ("fill'd" in line seven and "starv'd" in line nine are followed by the likes of "misus'd," "clip'd," "wand'ring," etc.), as the next poem shows, these may in fact not be prosodic apostrophes at all, but only orthographical habit. In any event, it seems clear that Blake does not care a good deal—or he would have made his specific intentions clear, as he was perfectly capable of doing.

m. *Of the Sleep of Ulro! and of the passage through*
Eternal Death! and of the awaking to Eternal Life.

This theme calls me in sleep night after night, and ev'ry
morn
Awakes me at sun-rise; then I see the Saviour over me.
Spreading his beams of love and dictating the words of
this mild song.   5

"Awake! awake O sleeper of the land of shadows,
wake! expand!
"I am in you and you in me, mutual in love divine:
"Fibres of love from man to man thro' Albion's
pleasant land.
"In all the dark Atlantic vale down from the hills of
Surrey
"A black water accumulates; return Albion! return!   10
"Thy brethren call thee, and thy fathers and thy sons,
"Thy nurses and thy mothers, thy sisters and thy
daughters
"Weep at thy soul's disease, and the Divine Vision is
darken'd,
"Thy Emanation that was wont to play before thy face,
"Beaming forth with her daughters into the Divine
bosom: 15
"Where hast thou hidden thy Emanation, lovely
Jerusalem,
"From the vision and fruition of the Holy-one?
"I am not a God afar off, I am a brother and friend:
"Within your bosoms I reside, and you reside in me:
"Lo! we are ONE, forgiving all Evil, Not seeking
recompense.   20
"Ye are my members, O ye sleepers of Beulah, land of
shades!" . . .
(Blake, *Jerusalem*, 1804 and after: excerpt)

Some of this can perhaps be read in Chaucerian-Compromise terms. But, so clearly is there no overall metrical pattern, in a

93

traditional sense, that the attempt at anything like scansion is futile. Not accidentally, a good deal of this moves and sounds remarkably like that later prosodic innovator, Walt Whitman. Blake's own explanation of his prosody in *Jerusalem* is set out as the second portion of a brief preface, the overall title of which is "To the Public." The prosodic explanation is headed "Of the Measure in which the following Poem is written."

> We who dwell on Earth can do nothing of ourselves; every thing is conducted by Spirits, no less than Digestion or Sleep . . .
> When this Verse was first dictated to me, I consider'd [*sic!*] a Monotonous Cadence, like that used by Milton and Shakespeare and all writers of English Blank Verse, derived from the modern bondage of Rhyming, to be a necessary and indispensible part of Verse. But I soon found that in the mouth of a true Orator such monotony was not only awkward, but as much a bondage as rhyme itself. I therefore have produced a variety in every line, both of cadences [i.e., stresses] and number of syllables. Every word and every letter is studied and put into its fit place; the terrific numbers are reserved for the terrific parts, the mild and gentle for the mild and gentle parts, and the prosaic for inferior parts; all are necessary to each other. Poetry Fetter'd Fetters the Human Race. Nations are Destroy'd or Flourish in proportion as Their Poetry, Painting and Music are Destroy'd or FLOURISH! The Primeval State of Man was Wisdom, Art and Science.

This is completely clear—and as we will see later, remarkably like the explanation Whitman offered for *his* innovative prosodic decisions. Though hardly evidence of insanity, it is also highly eccentric—one further reason for grouping Blake with Smart and Cowper. But unlike those earlier poets (thirty-five and twenty-six years his senior), Blake's eccentricities are not divergences from the typical educated gentleman's stance, but to a considerable extent fairly straightforward expressions of the common man's quite different way of living and thinking. Unlike virtually all the poets we have dealt with, of whose lives we know anything, Blake had not a trace of university education (or the set of aristocratic attitudes that almost invariably accompanied it). Without formal schooling of any kind, Blake (whose father was a hosier) became apprenticed to an engraver; he later attended the Royal Academy, but this was professional training, not comparable to the Oxbridge experience shared by most British poets before and even after his time. It can be argued that one powerful force enabling

Blake to break free of tradition, in all sorts of ways, was precisely his freedom from the conformities inculcated by higher education. (Whitman too was of a different and lower economic and social class from most American poets of his time.) Everything has its price; some advantages are dearly bought, and some apparent disadvantages can turn out to be path-clearing opportunities.

14 / The English Romantics

a.   five YEARS/ have PAST;/ five SUM/mers, WITH/ the
        LENGTH/
      of FIVE/ long WIN/ters! AND/ aGAIN/ i HEAR/
      these WA/ters, ROL/ling FROM/ their MOUN/tain
        SPRINGS/
      WITH a/ soft IN/land MUR/mur.—ONCE/ aGAIN/
      do I/ beHOLD/ these STEEP/ and LOF/ty CLIFFS,/   5
      that ON/ a WILD/ seCLUD/ed SCENE/ imPRESS/
      THOUGHTS of/ more DEEP/ seCLU/sion; AND/
        conNECT/
      the LAND/scape WITH/ the QUI/et OF/ the
        SKY./ . . .
            (William Wordsworth, "Lines Composed a Few Miles
                  Above Tintern Abbey," 1798: excerpt)

It has been noted by many commentators that Wordsworth's
poetic approach is pretty directly traceable to eighteenth-century
influences. This is hardly surprising, since he was born in 1770.
However innovative he may have been in matters substantive, in
prosody as in other matters of poetic technique he was throughout his long career as consistently conservative as, after the early
glow of radicalism had faded (it lasted about a decade), he became
in his social and religious views.

b. 'tis the MID/dle of NIGHT/ by the CAST/le CLOCK,/
    and the OWLS/ have aWA/kened the CROW/ing COCK;/

TU/—WHIT!/—TU/—WHOO!/
and HARK/, aGAIN!/ the CROW/ing COCK,/
how DROW/siLY/it CREW./   5
sir LE/oLINE,/ the BA/ron RICH,/
HATH/ a TOOTH/less MAS/tiff BITCH;/
FROM/ her KEN/nel beNEATH/ the ROCK/
she MA/keth AN/swer TO/ the CLOCK,/
FOUR for/ the QUAR/ters, and TWELVE/ for the HOur*;/ 10
Ever/ and AYE,/ by SHINE/ and SHOWer/
SIXteen/ short HOWLS,/ not O/ver LOUD;/
some SAY,/ she SEES/ my LA/dy's SHROUD./

IS the/ NIGHT /CHILly/ and DARK?/
the NIGHT/ is CHIL/ly, BUT/ not DARK./   15
the THIN/ gray CLOUD/ is SPREAD/ on HIGH,/
it CO/vers BUT/ not HIDES/ the SKY./
the MOON/ is beHIND,/ and AT/ the FULL;/
and YET/ she LOOKS/ both SMALL/ and DULL./
the NIGHT/ is CHILL,/ the CLOUD/ is GRAY:/   20
'tis a MONTH/ beFORE/ the MONTH/ of MAY,/
and the SPRING/ comes SLOW/ly UP/ this WAY./
                (Samuel Taylor Coleridge, "Christabel," 1797: excerpt)

*bisyllabic, to rhyme with "SHOWer"

Coleridge's prosody is remarkably like Wordsworth's, for the
most part, with an admixture of ballad- and folk-style poems in
which bi- and trisyllabic feet are blended pretty much indiscriminately, with the folkish trisyllabic predominating. "Answer to a
Child's Question" (1802), e.g., begins typically: "do you ASK/
what the BIRDS/ say? the SPAR/row, the DOVE,/ // the LIN/net
and THRUSH/ say i LOVE/ and i LOVE/." Accordingly, although Coleridge's prefatory note includes the assertion that
"the metre of Christabel is . . . founded on a new principle:
namely, that of counting in each line the accents, not the syllables," the facts are demonstrably that (a) "Christabel" is usually
either in pretty standard iambic tetrameter (and trimeter), with—
again—an admixture of bi- and trisyllabic feet, indiscriminately
blended, and (b) there is not much new in English prosody about
counting accents rather than syllables, even were that what
Coleridge is actually doing. But it is *not* what he is doing: line

three, with its four syllables, each accented, can thus be described, but I find no other similar line in the poem. (Indeed, when this replication of the owls calling is repeated, in lines three hundred and nine and three hundred and ten, traditional scansion is required: "from CLIFF/ and TOW/er, tu-WHOO!/ tu-WHOO!/ // tu-WHOO!/ tu-WHOO!/ from WOOD/ and FELL!" If we read this scansion back into line three, we would have to scan it in regular dimeter: "tu-WHIT!/ tu-WHOO!") Even line hundred and forty-one, though it too contains forceful exclamations, is in perfectly regular meter: "aLAS,/ aLAS!/ said GER/alDINE/". Inserted in a passage of fully trisyllabic feet (i.e., dactylic), we do find line two hundred and seventy-seven, but I cannot scan it by any of the meters used in the poem: "And didst bring her home with thee in love and in charity." (Coleridge's other assertion, in his his Preface, that "the metre of Christabel is not, properly speaking, irregular," is thus inaccurate as well.)

Like many of Coleridge's explanations, all his life long, his further assertion, as reported by Wordsworth, that he wrote "so little" . . . [because of] the extreme care and labour which he applied in elaborating his metres," is totally suspect. "He said," Wordsworth goes on, "that when he was intent on a new experiment in metre, the time and labour he bestowed were inconceivable; that he was quite an epicure in sound." (Quoted in *The Poems of Samuel Taylor Coleridge*, ed. Ernest Hartley Coleridge, London, Oxford University Press, 1912, p.511, n.1.) The small section —six pages, counting footnote material—devoted to "Metrical Experiments" in the six hundred and fourteen-page edition, just cited, of his complete poems, is I'm afraid simply the standard doodling of the classically educated Englishman, wistfully but futilely trying to force classical metrics on English. The little poem which George Saintsbury calls "admirable" trochaics (Ibid., p.516, n.2) is worth quoting in full, if only to show how a determined eye and ear will hear and see anything it has made up its mind to hear and see:

THUS/ she SAID,/ and, ALL/ aROUND,/
HER/ diVIN/er SPI/rit, GAN/ to BORrow;/
EAR/thly HEA/rings HEAR/ unEAR/thly SOUND,/
HEARTS/ heRO/ic FAINT,/ and SINK, aSWOUND./

WEL/come, WEL/come, SPITE/ of PAIN/ and SORrow,/   5
LOVE/ to-DAY,/ and THOUGHT/ to-MORrow./

To struggle successfully against the overwhelmingly dominant iambic movement of English is incredibly difficult. It can be managed, though seldom for as long as a complete line. But in a six-line poem supposedly in trochaics, how can we have the first, third, and fourth lines ending in (a) a resoundingly stressed syllable, and (b) a stressed syllable which, still worse, echoes heavily with its rhyme-freight? The rising movement of the lines themselves seems obvious to an unprejudiced ear.

c.   so we'll GO/ no MORE/ a ROving/
        so LATE/ INto/ the NIGHT,/
    though the HEART/ be STILL/ as LOving,/
    and the MOON/ be STILL/ as BRIGHT./

    for the SWORD/ outWEARS/ its SHEATH,/   5
    and the SOUL/ wears OUT/ the BREAST,/
  and the HEART/ must PAUSE/ to BREATHE,/
    and LOVE/ itSELF/ have REST./

  though the NIGHT/ was MADE/ for LOving,/
    and the DAY/ reTURNS/ too SOON,/   10
  yet we'll GO/ no MORE/ a ROving/
    by the LIGHT/ of the MOON./
        (George Gordon, Lord Byron,
   "So We'll Go No More A Roving," 1817)

Byron's deployment of the trisyllabic foot, here, is anything but random. It is used as the metric of the first foot in ten of the poem's twelve lines; it is used for feminine rhyme-endings, of which he was notoriously fond (and which he uses to such wickedly marvelous effect in *Don Juan*); and it is used, with great delicacy, to break the trimeter pattern, and thus end the poem, with the only totally trisyllabic (or dactylic) line in the poem. Indeed, of the two lines which do not begin with a trisyllabic foot, lines two and eight, only one, line eight, is in completely regular iambic trimeter—and the ear half sinks into its peaceful orderliness, beautifully complementing the line's substantive content: "and LOVE/ itSELF/ have REST."

d.   . . . brave MEN/ were LI/ving BE/fore A/gaMEMnon/
         and SINCE,/ exCEE/ding VA/loRUS/ and SAGE,/
    a GOOD/ deal LIKE/ him TOO,/ though QUITE/ the
         SAME none;/
         but THEN/ they SHONE/ not ON/ the PO/et's
         PAGE,/
    and SO/ have BEEN/ forGOT/ten:— I/ conDEMN
         none,/   5
         but CAN'T/ find A/ny IN/ the PRE/sent AGE/
    FIT for/ my PO/em (THAT/ is, FOR/ my NEW
         one);/
    so, AS/ i SAID,/ i'll TAKE/ my FRIEND/ don
         JUan./ . . .

    in SE/ville WAS/ he BORN,/ a PLEA/sant CIty,/
         FAmous/ for OR/anGES/ and WOmen—HE/   10
    who HAS/ not SEEN/ it WILL/ be MUCH/ to PIty,/
         so SAYS/ the PRO/verb—AND/ i QUITE/
         aGREE;/
    of ALL/ the SPAN/ish TOWNS/ is NONE/ more
         PRETty,/
         caDIZ/ perHAPS/—but THAT/ you SOON/ may
         SEE;/
    don JU/an's PA/rents LIVED/ beSIDE/ the RIver,/   15
    a NO/ble STREAM,/ and CALLED/ the
         GUA/dalQUIvir./

    his FA/ther's NAME/ was JO/se—*DON*,/
         of COURSE,—/
         a TRUE/ hiDAL/go, FREE/ from EVE/ry
         STAIN/
    of MOOR/ or HE/brew BLOOD,/ he TRACED/ his
         SOURCE/
         THROUGH the/ most GO/thic GEN/tleMEN/ of
         SPAIN;/   20

a BET/ter CA/vaLIER/ ne're MOUN/ted
    HORSE,/
    or, BE/ing MOUN/ted, E'ER/ got DOWN/
    aGAIN,/
than JO/se, WHO/ beGOT/ our HE/ro, WHO/
beGOT/—but THAT'S/ to COME—well, TO/
    reNEW:/ . . .
            (Byron, *Don Juan*, 1818, Canto One: excerpts)

From a prosodic point of view (surely not the major perspective
on so great a poem), *Don Juan*'s major significance is the very
intensity of Byron's *metrical* fooling about. We expect and want
slapdashery in a comic poem; Byron fills our cup, and to over-
flowing. Byron's personal poetic hero, Alexander Pope, pretty
much confined *his* fooling about to substantive and lexical matters: meter (like form) was for him essentially inviolate. Born
exactly a century after Pope, Byron's poetic ear was inevitably
differently shaped—and as we will see, his disciplined (but no
less restless, despite their discipline) excursions into metrical
variety comport well with the still greater metrical divergences
that are to be found in the work of his younger contemporaries,
Shelley (4 years his junior) and Keats (7 years his junior).

e.   the AW/ful SHA/dow OF/ some UN/seen POWer/
        FLOATS though/ unSEEN/ aMONG/ us,—
        VI/siTING/
    this VA/rious WORLD/ with AS/ inCON/stant
        WING/
    as SUM/mer WINDS/ that CREEP/ from FLOW/er to
        FLOWer.*/
    like MOON/beams THAT/ beHIND/ some PI/ny
        MOUN/tain SHOWer,/   5
        it VIsits WITH/ inCON/stant GLANCE/
        each HU/man HEART/ and COUN/teNANCE;/
    like HUES/ and HAR/moNIES/ of EV/enING,—†/
        like CLOUDS/ in STAR/light WIDE/ly
        SPREAD,—/
        like ME/moRY/ of MU/sic FLED,—/   10
        like AUGHT/ that FOR/ its GRACE/ may BE/
    DEAR and/ yet DEAR/er FOR/ its MY/steRY./

SPIRit/ of BEAU/ty, THAT/ dost CON/seCRATE/
    with THINE/ own HUES/ all THOU/ dost
    SHINE/ upON/
    of HU/man THOUGHT/ or FORM,/—where
    ART/ thou GONE?/   15
why DOST/ thou PASS/ aWAY/ and LEAVE/ our
    STATE/
this DIM/ vast VALE/ of TEARS,/ VAcant/ and
    DE/soLATE?†/
    ask WHY/ the SUN/light NOT/ for Ever/
    weaves RAIN/bows O'ER/ yon MOUN/tain-RIver,/
why AUGHT/ should FAIL/ and FADE/ that ONCE/
    is SHOWN,/   20
    why FEAR/ and DREAM/ and DEATH/ and
    BIRTH/
    CAST on/ the DAY/light OF/ this EARTH/
    such GLOOM,/—why MAN/ has SUCH/ a SCOPE/
for LOVE/ and HATE,/ desPON/denCY/ and
    HOPE?/

no VOICE/ from SOME/ subLI/mer WORLD/ hath
    Ever/   25
    to SAGE/ or PO/et, THESE/ reSPON/ses
    GIven—/
    THEREfore/ the NAMES/ of DAE/mon,
    GHOST,/ and HEAven,/
reMAIN/ the RE/cords OF/ their VAIN/ enDEAvor,/
frail SPELLS/—whose UT/tered CHARM/ might
    NOT/ aVAIL/ to SEver,/
    from ALL/ we HEAR/ and ALL/ we SEE,/   30
    doubt, CHANCE,/ and MU/taBI/liTY./
thy LIGHT/ aLONE/—like MIST/ o'er MOUN/tains
    DRIven,/
    or MU/sic BY/ the NIGHT/-wind SENT/
    through STRINGS/ of SOME/ still IN/struMENT,/
    or MOON/light ON/ a MID/night STREAM,/   35
gives GRACE/ and TRUTH, to LIFE'S/ unQUI/et
    DREAm./ . . .
    (Percy Bysshe Shelley, "Hymn to Intellectual Beauty,"
                    1816: excerpt)

---

*bisyllabic, to rhyme with "SHOWer"
†trisyllabic, to rhyme with "WING"

For a poet of pre-eminently lyric gifts, this is, prosodically, an oddly stiff poem. In the first thirty-six lines, here cited, there are nine metrical feet in which the stress falls on brief particles, short monosyllables which rarely acquire either metrical or linguistics stress (lines one, three, five, six, eleven, twelve, thirteen, twenty-two, and twenty-eight). "Of" is metrically stressed three times, "for" and "that" twice each. I have not counted "stronger" monosyllables like "be, art, why, not, o'er, all, by," not to mention longer and stronger monosyllables like "floats, wing, creep," and so on. Further: there are eight instances of somewhat unnatural stretching out of polysyllabic words, the meter plainly requiring that each and every syllable be given full metrical weight (lines two, seven, eight, ten, twelve, thirteen, seventeen, and thirty-one). These are unusually high incidences of what we might suspect to be casual, even indifferent (i.e., uncaring) metrical practice. Further examples of Shelley's verse show, not surprisingly (considering, that is, Byron's practice and the sometimes folkishly relaxed prosody of Coleridge), that not only in Shelley, but also in the work of John Keats, casual, even indifferent metrical practice is exactly what we find.

f. o WILD/ west WIND,/ thou BREATH/ of AU/tumn's
        BEing,/
      THOU, from/ whose UN/seen PRE/sence *the leaves dead*
      are DRI/ven, like GHOSTS/ from AN/ enCHAN/ter
        FLEEing,/

      YELlow, and BLACK,/ and PALE,/ and HEC/tic RED,/
      PESti'lence/-STRIC/ken MUL/tiTUDES/: o THOU,/   5
      who CHA/rioTEST/ to THEIR/ dark WIN/try BED/

      the WIN/ged SEEDS,/ where THEY/ lie COLD/ and
        LOW,/
      each LIKE/ a CORPSE/ withIN/ its GRAVE,/ unTIL/
      thine AZ/ure SIS/ter OF/ the SPRING/ shall BLOW/

      her CLA/rion O'ER/ the DREA/ming EARTH,/ and
        FILL/   10
      (DRIving/ sweet BUDS/ like FLOCKS/ to FEED/ in AIR)/
      with LIV/ing HUES/ and O/dours [,] PLAIN/ and HILL:/

wild SPI/rit, WHICH/ art MO/ving EVE/ryWHERE,/
deSTROY/er AND/ preSER/ver; HEAR,/ oh, HEAR!/
(Shelley, "Ode to the West Wind," 1819: excerpt)

The portion of line two which I have marked as more or less
unscannable is, unfortunately, probably to be scanned as "THE/
leaves DEAD," which makes no linguistic and precious little
metrical sense. That is, the distance between linguistically permissible stresses and designated metrical stresses is so large that,
essentially, they here bear no relationship the one to the other.
Put differently: the poem's metrical standard is abstract rather
than founded in the language. Put still differently: there can be
none of the invaluable tension between the two standards, linguistic and metrical, which over the centuries has vitally enriched the
music of English verse. The less striking but still linguistically
rather absurd metrical readings imposed on line six adds to one's
conviction that all is starting to go much less well with the
Chaucerian Compromise: both "CHA/rioTEST/" and "THEIR/
dark WIN/try" are at best mechanical, at worst linguistically
unnatural rhythms. The signal fact is that neither Shelley nor any
of his critics, then or now, seem to mind. They seem to expect
these freedoms from verse at this point in the history of English
poetry.

g.　HAIL/ to THEE,/ blithe SPI/rit!/
　　　BIRD/ thou NE/ver WERT,/
　　THAT/ from HEA/ven, or NEAR it,/
　　　POU/rest THY/ full HEART/
　　in PRO/fuse STRAINS/ of UN/preME/diTA/ted
　　　　ART./   5

　　HIGH/er STILL/ and HIGHer/
　　　FROM/ the EARTH/ thou SPRINGest/
　　LIKE/ a CLOUD/ of FIre;*/
　　　the blue deep /thou WINGest,/
　　and SING/ing STILL/ dost SOAR,/ and SOAR/ing E/ver
　　　SINGest./   10

　　IN/ the GOL/den LIGHTning/
　　　OF/ the SUN/ken SUN,/

O'ER/ which CLOUDS/ are BRIGHT'ning,/
   THOU/ dost FLOAT/ and RUN;/
LIKE an/ unBO/died JOY/ whose RACE/ is JUST/
   beGUN./   15

The pale PUR/ple Even/
   MELTS/ aROUND/ thy FLIGHT;/
LIKE/ a STAR/ of HEAven,/
   IN/ the BROAD/ dayLIGHT/
thou ART/ unSEEN,/ but YET/ i HEAR/ thy
   SHRILL/ deLIGHT./   20

KEEN/ as ARE/ the ARrows/
   OF/ that SIL/ver SPHERE,/
WHOSE/ inTENSE/ lamp NARrows/
   IN/ the WHITE/ dawn CLEAR/
unTIL/ we HARD/ly SEE/—we FEEL/ that IT/ is
   THERE./   25

ALL/ the EARTH/ and AIR/
   WITH/ thy VOICE/ is LOUD,/
AS,/ when NIGHT/ is BARE,/
   FROM/ one LONE/ly CLOUD/
the MOON/ rains OUT/ her BEAMS,/ and
   HEA/ven is O/verFLOWED./ . . .
                 (Shelley, "To a Skylark," 1820: excerpt)

---

*"fire" must be—unnaturally—bisyllabic in order to rhyme with
"HIGHer"

Lines nine and sixteen are not in fact in any way doubtful as to
scansion: I have so marked them only because it is hard (though
necessary) to believe what Shelley has here done. In the light of
the elaborately maintained replicative prosodic pattern (the poem
is over one hundred lines in length, and Shelley puts an invariable
initial metrical stress in each of the four trimeter lines, as he
makes the fifth line of each stanza hexameter), line nine can *only*
be scanned "THE/ blue DEEP/ thou WINGest,/" and line sixteen
can *only* be scanned "THE/ pale PUR/ple Even/". The linguistic
absurdity of these scansions needs no underlining—but then,
who in nineteenth-century England could possibly have said

"PROfuse" instead of "proFUSE" (line five), or "dayLIGHT" instead of "DAYlight" (line nineteen)? The metrical stresses on "in" and "of," in lines eleven and twelve, and lines twenty-two and twenty-four, are clear, but what relationship do they have to the linguistic facts of the language? Line twenty may well be meant to be scanned, at the start, "thou ART," rather than, as here, the more natural "THOU art" —but in a sense, what earthly difference does it make? Scansion is an abstract, almost a meaningless game, when one employs it as Shelley does. We do not care whether we scan "THOU art" or "thou ART" because it is clear that the poet does not care. (Asked whether this note or that one was to be accented, the composer Frederick Delius replied, "Any way you like, dear boy.") The important thing is that, since the poet's ear no longer pays much attention to the once viable artificialities of the Chaucerian Compromise, neither does his poem.

h.   *Scansion A*   *Scansion B*

WHEN/ the LAMP/ is   when the LAMP/ is
SHATtered   SHATtered/
the LIGHT/ in the DUST/   [SAME]
lies DEAD—/
WHEN/ the CLOUD/ is   when the CLOUD/ is
SCATtered/   SCATtered/
the RAIN/bow's GLO/ry is   [SAME]
SHED./
WHEN/ the LUTE/ is   when the LUTE/ is   5
BROken,/   BROken,/
sweet TONES/ are reMEM/   [SAME]
bered NOT;/
WHEN/ the LIPS/ have   when the LIPS/ have
SPOken,/   SPOken,/
loved AC/cents are SOON/   [SAME]
forGOT./

AS/ MUsic/ and SPLEN-   as MU/sic and SPLEN-
dor/   dor/
surVIVE/ not the LAMP/   [SAME]   10
and the LUTE,/

106

the HEART'S/ ECHoes/
    RENder/
no SONG/ when the SPI/rit
    is MUTE:—/
NO/ song BUT/ sad
    DIRges,/
like the WIND/ through a
    RU/ined CELL,/
OR/ the MOURN/ful
    SURges/
that RING/ the DEAD/ sea-
    man's KNELL./
WHEN/ hearts HAVE/
    once MINgled/

love FIRST/ leaves the
    WELL/-built NEST;/
THE/ weak ONE/ is
    SINgled/
to enDURE/ what it ONCE/
    posSESSED./
o LOVE!/ WHO/
    beWAIlest/
the FRAIL/ity* of ALL/
    things HERE,/
WHY/ choose YOU/ the
    FRAILest/
for your CRAD/le, your
    HOME,/ and your
    BIER?/

ITS/ PASsions/ will ROCK
    thee/
as the STORMS/ rock the
    RA/vens on HIGH;/
BRIGHT/ REAson/ will
    MOCK thee,/
like the SUN/ from a WIN/
    try SKY./
FROM/ thy NEST/ every
    RAFter/

the HEART'S/ echoes
    RENder/
NO song/ WHEN the/ SPIrit/
    is MUTE:—/
no SONG/ but sad
    DIRges./
[SAME]

or the MOURN/ful   15
    SURges/
[SAME]

when HEARTS/ have
    once MINgled/

LOVE/ first LEAVES/ the
    WELL/-built NEST,/
the WEAK/ one is
    SINgled/
[SAME]   20

o LOVE!/ who
    beWAIlest/
the FRA/ilTY†/ of ALL/
    things HERE,/
why CHOOSE/ you the
    FRAILest/
[SAME]

its PAS/sions will ROCK   25
    thee/
AS/ the STORMS/ rock the
    RA/vens on HIGH;/
bright REA/son will
    MOCK thee,/
[SAME]

from thy NEST/ every
    RAFter/

107

will ROT,/ and thine EA/gle	[SAME]
HOME/	
LEAVE/ thee NA/ked to	leave thee NA/ked to
LAUGHter/	LAUGHter/

30

when leaves fall and cold
   winds come.
        (Shelley, "Lines: When the Lamp is Shattered," 1822)

---

*bisyllabic
†trisyllabic

It would be hard (and I think impossible) to find a poem from the Golden Age of the Chaucerian Compromise which, as here, could be given such disparate scansions, all with about an equal show of logic and consistency, all founded in much the same reading of the poet's prior and contemporary poems. I have marked the wonderfully uncertain final line as perhaps more uncertain than it in fact is, to emphasize the point. The metrical pattern, to the extent it is comprehensible (or that it exists), seems to require a trimeter final line, mostly anapestic, in each stanza. Thus: "when LEAVES/ fall and COLD/ winds COME./" This however obviously runs hard against the linguistic grain; the line can be scanned in this way only by forcing the metrical reading on the natural, linguistic one. But there are *two* alternative possibilities, both tetrameter: "when LEAVES/ FALL/ and COLD/ winds COME/" *or* "WHEN leaves/ FALL/ and COLD/ winds COME." And I find no dispositive reason to favor either of these tetrameter scansions over the other. We are left, accordingly, with three possible scansions, and no definitive way of deciding between and among them.

And, after closely studying the metrical behavior exhibited in this poem, if we have not virtually defined the imminent breakdown of the Chaucerian Compromise, I do not know how better to define it.

i. SEAson/ of MISTS/ and MEL/low FRUIT/fulNESS,/
   close BO/som-FRIEND/ of THE/ maTUR/ing SUN;/
conSPIR/ing WITH/ him HOW/ to LOAD/ and BLESS/
   with FRUIT/ the VINES/ that ROUND/ the
      THATCH/-eaves RUN;/

to BEND/ with AP/ples THE/ mossed COT/tage-TREES,/ 5
 and FILL/ all FRUIT/ with RIPE/ness TO/ the CORE;/
  to SWELL/ the GOURD,/ and
  PLUMP/ the HA/zel SHELLS
WITH a/ sweet KER/nel; TO/ set BUD/ding MORE,/
and STILL/ more, LAT/er FLOW/ers FOR/ the BEES,/
unTIL/ they THINK/ warm DAYS/ will NE/ver CEASE,/ 10
  for SUM/mer HAS/ o'er-BRIMM'D/
  their CLAM/my CELLS./

who HATH/ not SEEN/ thee OFT/ aMID/ thy STORE?/
 SOMEtimes/ whoE/ver SEEKS/ aBROAD/ may FIND/
thee SIT/ting CARE/less ON/ a GRA/nary FLOOR,/
thy HAIR soft-LIFT/ed BY/ the WIN/nowing WIND;/ 15
or ON/ a HALF/-reap'd FUR/row SOUND/ aSLEEP,/
 DROWSED with/ the FUME/ of POP/pies, WHILE/
  thy HOOK/
  SPARES the/ next SWATH/ and
  ALL/ its TWIN/ed FLOWers:/
and SOME/times LIKE/ a GLEAN/er THOU/ dost KEEP/
STEAdy/ thy LA/den HEAD/ aCROSS/ a BROOK;/ 20
or BY/ a CI/der-PRESS,/ with PA/tient LOOK,/
  thou WATCH/est the LAST/
  OOZings,/ HOUrs*/ by HOUrs.*/

WHERE are/ the SONGS/ of SPRING?/ aye, WHERE/
 are THEY?/
 think NOT/ of THEM,/ thou HAST/ thy
 MU/sic TOO,—/
while BAR/red CLOUDS/ BLOOM the/ soft-DY/ing DAY,/ 25
 and TOUCH/ the STUB/ble-PLAINS/ with
 RO/sy HUE;/
THEN in/ a WAIL/ful CHOIR/ the SMALL/ gnats
 MOURN/
aMONG/ the RI/ver SAL/lows, BORNE/ aLOFT/
  or SINK/ing AS/ the LIGHT/ wind
 LIVES/ or DIES;/

and FULL/-grown LAMBS/ loud BLEAT/ from
    HIL/ly BORN;/   30
hedge-CRIC/kets SING;/ and NOW/ with
    TRE/ble SOFT/
the RED/breast WHIST/les FROM/ a
    GAR/den-CROFT,/
        and GA/thering SWAL/lows TWIT/ter
IN/ the SKIES./

                                (John Keats, "To Autumn," 1819)

---

*bisyllabic, to rhyme with "FLOWers"

Much that we have already seen in Shelley is more or less repeated, here. The exceedingly strange scansion of line twenty-two can only be avoided by another scansion equally strange—or perhaps somewhat stranger: "thou WATCH/est THE/ last OOZ/ ings, HOURS/ by HOUrs./" (At least, this scansion allows the first iteration of "hours" to be naturally monosyllabic; it is also true that, in a terminal position, with a syntactic closure following, "hours" is somewhat more justifiably bisyllabic, because naturally longer.) The faintly astonishing thing to note is that this alternative scansion, which would place a linguistically absurd metrical stress on "the," is metrically almost unavoidable in not one but arguably two earlier lines of this same poem, namely, lines two and five. If "the" is not stressed in line two, it becomes—impossibly—a tetrameter rather than, as plainly required, a pentameter line. And the only way out of metrically stressing "the" in line five is this scansion: "to BEND/ with AP/ ples the MOSSED/ COT/tage-TREES." This is five stresses, to be sure. But what metrical pattern does it follow?

Perhaps the clearest way to understanding what Keats is really up to, prosodically, and how differently his poetic ear functions within the nominal bounds of the Chaucerian Compromise, is to take the poem, line by line, and (a) count up how many natural linguistic stresses occur and (b) study their positioning. There is no need to thus analyze the entire poem; I think we can see all we need to from just the first stanza:

line 1   4 linguistic stresses; syllables 1, 4, 6, 8
line 2   5 linguistic stresses; syllables 1, 2, 4, 8, 10
line 3   4 linguistic stresses; syllables 2, 6, 8, 10

110

line 4   6 linguistic stresses; syllables 2, 4, 6, 8, 9, 10
line 5   5 linguistic stresses; syllables 2, 4, 7, 8, 10
line 6   4 linguistic stresses; syllables 2, 4, 6, 10
line 7   5 linguistic stresses; syllables 2, 4, 6, 8, 10
line 8   5 linguistic stresses; syllables 3, 4, 7, 8, 10
line 9   5 linguistic stresses; syllables 2, 3, 4, 6, 10
line 10   7 linguistic stresses; syllables 2, 3, 4, 5, 6, 8, 10
line 11   4 linguistic stresses; syllables 2, 6, 8, 10

There may be some difference in different people's counts, here; not everyone, perhaps, would find seven linguistic stresses in line ten. But even if we drop, arguendo, the linguistic stress on "they," which is the third syllable in the line, *there is only one line of the first eleven—line seven—in which the positioning of the natural linguistic stresses coincides with the positioning of metrical stresses in a standard iambic pentameter Chaucerian Compromise line.* This is simple, stark fact; it cannot be explained away. And it speaks loudly, as well as volumes-worth. Readers whose ears have been trained by the very different prosodies of the twentieth century find it extremely hard to accept the notion that Keats and his contemporaries were indeed serious about a prosodic system to which, in plain actuality, they paid so little attention. And, in a word, they are right. The fundamental support which upholds any cultural agreement is collective belief and assent. That faith, if you will, need not be unanimous. But it must be strong before it can be enduring. In late 1990, as I write these words, we are seeing just how true that statement is, on a genuinely macrocosmic scale, and all across the globe. Governments and governmental systems lacking strong collective belief and assent are in fact toppling virtually right and left (no pun intended). If the sickle-and-hammer power structure of Lenin and Stalin and their heirs, three-quarters of a century old, cannot resist basic cultural forces, what could make us expect any different fate for a cultural agreement intrinsically much less powerful?

Moribund systems can of course recoup, can struggle into second-effort positions from which they are able to survive. We are seeing that, too, across the globe—and on the whole unfortunately—in late 1990. The Chaucerian Compromise was increasingly moribund through the entire nineteenth century. But by 1990, if no longer dominant, if no longer ever again to be the only game in town, the Chaucerian Compromise had taken on new life and strength.

But, once again, we must not too much anticipate what the historical record is about to tell us.

15 / American Poets
Before Whitman

a. WHIther,/ midst FAL/ling DEW,/
while GLOW/ the HEA/vens WITH/ the last STEPS/ of
   DAY,/
FAR, through/ their RO/sy DEPTHS,/ dost THOU/
   purSUE/
   thy SO/liTA/ry WAY?/

VAINly/ the FOW/lers EYE/   5
might MARK/ thy DIS/tant FLIGHT,/ to DO/ thee
   WRONG,/
as, DARK/ly SEEN/ aGAINST/ the CRIM/son SKY,/
   thy FI/gure FLOATS/ aLONG./

SEEK'ST thou/ the PLA/shy BRINK/
of WEE/dy LAKE,/ or MARGE/ of RI/ver WIDE,/   10
or WHERE/ the ROCK/ing BIL/lows RISE/ and SINK/
   on the CHAF/ed O/cean SIDE?/

THERE is/ a POW/er, whose CARE/
TEAches/ thy WAY/ aLONG/ that PATH/less COAST,—/
the DE/sert AND/ ilLI/miTA/ble AIR,/   15
   lone WAN/dering, BUT/ not LOST./ . . .
   (William Cullen Bryant, "To a Waterfowl," 1829: excerpt)

America's first professional poet, Bryant was frequently at-
tacked—in the United States—for indulging in trisyllabic feet. As

we have seen, the British poets on whom he so plainly modelled himself did pretty much the same thing. To be sure, as these lines show, they did it better.

b. how MUCH,/ preVEN/ting GOD!/ how MUCH/ i OWE/
TO the/ deFEN/ses THOU/ hast ROUND/ me SET:/
exAM/ple, CUS/tom, FEAR,/ ocCAS/ion SLOW,/
these SCOR/ned BONDS/men WERE/ my PA/raPET./
i DARE/ not PEEP/ Over/ this PA/raPET/   5
to GAUGE/ with GLANCE/ the ROAR/ing GULF/ beLOW,/
the DEPTHS/ of SIN/ to WHICH/ i HAD/ deSCENded,/
had NOT/ these ME/ aGAINST/ mySELF/ deFENded./
        (Ralph Waldo Emerson, "Grace," 1842)

Stiff and clumsy, the music of this poem sounds for all the world like the literary lessons learned by a hardworking foreigner, one for whom English was a learned rather than a native tongue. But as a prosodist (and as a poet), Thoreau was even worse:

c.   great GOD,/ i ASK/ for THEE/ no MEA/ner PELF/
than THAT/ i MAY/ not DI/sapPOINT/ mySELF,/
that IN/ my AC/tion I/ may SOAR/ as HIGH/
as I/ can NOW/ disCERN/ with THIS/ clear EYE./

and NEXT/ in VA/lue, WHICH/ thy KIND/ness
   LENDS,/   5
that I/ may GREAT/ly DI/sapPOINT/ my
   FRIENDS,/
howE'ER/ they THINK/ or HOPE/ that IT/ may
   BE,/
they MAY/ not DREAM/ how THOU'ST/
   disTIN/guished ME./ . . .
      (Henry David Thoreau, "Prayer," 1842: excerpt)

d.   the SKIES/ they were ASH/en and SOber;/
the LEAVES/ they were CRIS/ped and SERE—/
the LEAVES/ they were WI/thering* and SERE:/
it was NIGHT,/ in the LONE/some ocTOber/
of my MOST/ immeMO/rial YEAR:/   5

it was HARD/ by the DIM/ lake of AUber,/
   in the MIS/ty mid RE/gion of WEIR—/
it was DOWN/ by the DANK/ tarn of AUber,/
   in the GHOST/-haunted WOOD/land of WEIR./ . . .
       (Edgar Allan Poe, "Ulalume," 1847: excerpt)

---

*probably bisyllabic

e.   how STRANGE/ it SEEMS!/ these HE/brews IN/ their
       GRAVES,/
       CLOSE by/ the STREET/ of THIS/ fair SEA/port
       TOWN,/
   SIlent/ beSIDE/ the NE/ver SI/lent WAVES,/
       at REST/ in ALL/ this MO/ving UP/ and DOWN!/

   the TREES/ are WHITE/ with DUST,/ that O'ER/ their
       SLEEP/
       WAVE their/ broad CUR/tains IN/ the
       SOUTH/wind's BREATH,/
   while UN/derNEATH/ these LEA/fy TENTS/ they
       KEEP/
       the LONG, mySTE/rious EX/oDUS/ of DEATH./

   and THESE/ sePUL/chral STONES,/ so OLD/ and
       BROWN,/
       that PAVE/ with LE/vel FLAGS/ their BU/rial
       PLACE,/
   SEEM like/ the TAB/lets OF/ the LAW,/ thrown
       DOWN/
       and BRO/ken by MO/ses AT/ the MOUN/tain's
       BASE./

   the VE/ry NAMES/ reCOR/ded HERE/ are
       STRANGE,/
       of FO/reign AC/cent, AND/ of DIF/ferent
       CLIMES;/
   alVA/res AND/ riVE/ra IN/terCHANGE/
       with AB/raHAM/ and JA/cob OF/ old TIMES./ . . .
   (Henry Wadsworth Longfellow, "The Jewish Cemetery at
             Newport, 1852: excerpt)

10

15

115

f.   i LOVE/ the OLD/ meLO/dious LAYS/
which SOFT/ly MELT/ the A/ges THROUGH,/
the SONGS/ of SPEN/ser's GOL/den DAYS,/
arCA/dian SID/ney's SIL/very PHRASE./
SPRINKling/ our NOON/ of TIME/ with FRE/shest
    MOR/ning DEW./   5

yet, VAIN/ly IN/ my QUI/et HOUrs*/
to BREATHE/ their MAR/velous NOTES/ i TRY;/
i FEEL/ them, AS/ the LEAVES/ and FLOWers/
in SI/lence FEEL/ the DE/wy SHOWers,/
and DRINK/ with GLAD/ still LIPS/ the BLES/sing OF/
    the SKY./   10

the RI/gor OF/ a FRO/zen CLIME,/
the HARSH/ness OF/ an UN/taught EAR,/
the JAR/ring WORDS/ of ONE/ whose RHYME/
beat OF/ten LA/bor's HUR/ried TIME,/
or DU/ty's RUG/ged MARCH through STORM and
    STRIFE,/ are HERE./   15

of MYS/tic BEAU/ty, DREA/my GRACE,/
no ROUN/ded ART/ the LACK/ supPLIES;/
unSKILLED/ the SUB/tle LINES/ to TRACE,/
or SOF/ter SHADES/ of NA/ture's FACE,/
i VIEW/ her COM/mon FORMS/ with UN/anNOIN/ted
    EYES./   20

nor MINE/ the SEER/-like POW/er to SHOW/
the SE/crets OF/ the HEART/ and MIND;/
to DROP/ the PLUM/met-LINE/ beLOW/
our COM/mon WORLD/ of JOY/ and WOE,/
a MORE/ inTENSE/ desPAIR/ or BRIGH/ter HOPE/
    to FIND./ . . .   25
           (John Greenleaf Whittier, "Proem," 1847: excerpt)

*bisyllabic, to rhyme with "FLOWers" and "SHOWers"

g.   THIS is/ the SHIP/ of PEARL,/ which, PO/ets
      FEIGN,/
    SAILS the/ unSHA/dowed MAIN,/

the VEN/turous BARK/ that FLINGS/
ON the/ sweet SUM/mer WIND/ its PUR/pled WINGS/
in GULFS/ enCHAN/ted, WHERE/ the SI/ren SINGS,/   5
   and CO/ral REEFS/ lie BARE,/
WHERE the/ cold SEA/-maids RISE/ to SUN/ their
   STREAM/ing HAIR./

its WEBS/ of LIV/ing GAUZE/ no MORE/ unFURL;/
   WRECKED is/ the SHIP/ of PEARL!/
   and EVE/ry CHAM/bered CELL,/   10
WHERE its/ dim DREAM/ing LIFE/ was WONT/ to
   DWELL,/
AS the/ frail TEN/ant SHAPED/ his GROW/ing
   SHELL,/
beFORE/ thee LIES/ reVEALED,/
its IR/ised CEIL/ing RENT,/ its SUN/less CRYPT/
   unSEALED!/ . . .
(Oliver Wendell Holmes, "The Chambered Nautilus," 1858:
excerpt)

None of these poets is exceptional or exceptionable; prosodically, too, they are competent but fairly dull copies of their
British models. Most of the metrical irregularities and variations
to be found in the poems discussed in the previous section, "The
English Romantics," are to be found here, essentially unchanged
though, once again, less melodious.

16 / *Tennyson, Browning, Swinburne, Hardy, Bridges*

a. BREAK,/ BREAK,/ BREAK,/
      on thy COLD/ gray STONES,/ o SEA!/
    and i WOULD/ that my TONGUE/ could UTter/
      the THOUGHTS/ that aRISE/ in me./

    o, WELL/ for the FISH/erman's BOY,/   5
      that he SHOUTS/ with his SIS/ter at PLAY!/
    o, WELL/ for the SAI/lor LAD,/
      that he SINGS/ in his BOAT/ on the BAY!/

    and the STATE/ly SHIPS/ go ON/
      to their HA/ven UN/der the HILL;/   10
    but O/ for the TOUCH/ of a VA/nished HAND,/
      and the SOUND/ of a VOICE/ that is STILL!/

    BREAK,/ BREAK,/ BREAK,/
      at the FOOT/ of thy CRAGS,/ o SEA!/
    but the TEN/der GRACE/ of a DAY/ that is DEAD/   15
      will NE/ver come BACK/ to me./
    (Alfred, Lord Tennyson, "Break, Break, Break," 1834)

Of primary prosodic significance, in the historical terms here being considered, are the following principal facts:

1) In traditional Chaucerian Compromise verse, lines one and thirteen would be scanned as two rather than three metrical feet: "BREAK,/ break, BREAK."

118

2) Other than the plainly aberrant lines one and thirteen, the poem contains fourteen lines, with a total of forty-seven metrical feet, of which well over half are trisyllabic. It is not the simple presence of an abundance of trisyllablic feet alone which is significant, however, but the constant but irregular (i.e., ad libitum) alternation of trisyllabic and bisyllabic. In a word, this prevents *any* pattern from being established. If we like, we can say with a flourish that, apart from lines one and thirteen, the poem is 57.45 percent anapestic, and 42.55 percent iambic. But saying that, what have we said, considering that there is no observable or predictable pattern to the alternation?

Taken as a whole, indeed, rather than a poem which is roughly half anapestic and half iambic, what we have is a poem which refuses to be *either* anapestic *or* iambic. Except for lines eleven and fifteen—of which more in a moment—the poem has three stresses per line, plus however many unstressed syllables the poet's ear desires. It almost does not make sense to call the metrical divisions in such a poem "feet": in effect, they are actually stress-clusters of shifting length (mono-, bi-, or trisyllabic)—and there is no need to underline what prosodic system that begins to resemble. (Though Old English alliteration is not to be found, here, lines one and thirteen rather closely resemble it and, in addition, there is significant alliteration in eight of the poem's other fourteen lines—counting the [k] in "cold" and the [g] in "gray," in line two, as alliterative.)

3) In the larger prosodic context just outlined, the fact that the third line in stanzas one and two is trimeter, but in stanzas three and four becomes tetrameter, is more than a merely incidental detail. That is, though Tennyson is clearly writing in stanza form, these are not fully replicative stanzas: indeed, *no stanza in the poem is metrically identical to any other stanza.* In the historical continuum we have been examining, this is a fact of major importance.

b.   the SPLEN/dour FALLS/ on CAS/tle WALLS/
      and SNO/wy SUM/mits OLD/ in STOry;/
      the LONG/ light SHAKES/ aCROSS/ the
          LAKES,/
      AND the/ wild CA/taract LEAPS/ in GLOry./

blow, bugle, blow, SET/ the wild ECH/oes FLYing,/   5
BLOW,/ BUgle;/ ANswer,/ ECHoes,/ DYing,/
DYing,/ DYing./ . . .

(Tennyson, *The Princess*: "The
Splendor Falls," 1850: excerpt)

The beginning of line five is not in fact in doubt, I think. I have
so marked it, once again, to underline the point that, though
traditional Chaucerian Compromise verse would scan two metrical feet, here ("BLOW,/ bugle, BLOW"), Tennyson pretty clearly
wants three ("BLOW,/ BUgle,/ BLOW"). Both the previous
poem and the succeeding line of this poem seem to plainly so
require.

Note that, although the poem is heavily rhymed (French influence), five of the six lines in this stanza are also markedly
alliterative (somewhat disguised in line four but palpable nonethe-
less).

c.   dark HOUSE, by WHICH/ once MORE/ i STAND/
    HERE in/ the LONG/ unLOVE/ly STREET,/
    DOORS, where/ my HEART/ was USED/ to BEAT/
so QUICK/ly, WAIT/ing FOR/ a HAND,/

a HAND/ that CAN/ be CLASPED/ no MORE —/   5
    beHOLD/ me, FOR/ i CAN/not SLEEP,/
    and LIKE/ a GUIL/ty THING/ i CREEP/
at EARL/iest MOR/ning TO/ the DOOR./

HE is/ not HERE;/ but FAR/ aWAY/
    the NOISE/ of LIFE/ beGINS/ aGAIN,/   10
    and GHAST/ly THROUGH/ the DRIZ/zling RAIN/
on the bald street breaks the blank day.

(Tennyson, *In Memoriam*, Poem 7, 1833–50)

These are not only elaborately replicative stanzas—quatrain-
form, all rhyming A B B A, with the second and third lines
consistently indented to emphasize the rhyming pattern—but
lines one through eleven are without exception in fairly regular
iambic tetrameter. Line twelve, which must be expected to

120

conform to the tight patterning, contains a total of eight syllables; this would ordinarily be exactly what was required for an iambic tetrameter line. But this is *not* an iambic line, whatever its arrangement. Do we scan "on" as having metrical stress: "ON the/ bald STREET/ BREAKS the/ blank DAY/"? This is probably prosodically most likely Tennyson's intention. Unfortunately, however, the linguistic ordering of the line requires not four but five stresses—and none of them fall on "on": "on the BALD STREET BREAKS the BLANK DAY." We have already seen that Tennyson is not only well aware of such arrangements of linguistic stress, but in fact uses them in his poetry. Given such an underlying linguistic ordering, to accommodate the prosodic scheme even as approximately as we have (scanning "on" with metrical stress), we have inevitably completely broken with the natural, linguistic ordering. Again, if this is as I suspect what Tennyson wanted, it plainly marks yet another nail in the Chaucerian Compromise's coffin.

d. o MIGH/ty-MOUTHED/ inVEN/tor of HAR/moNIES,/
    o SKILLED/ to SING/ of TIME/ or eTER/niTY,/
    god-GIF/ted OR/gan-VOICE/ of ENGland,/
    MILton,/ a NAME/ to reSOUND/ for Ages;/
    whose TI/tan AN/gels, GA/briEL,/ abDIEL*,/   5
    STARRED from/ jeHO/vah's GOR/geous AR/moRIES,/
    TOWer/ as the DEEP/-domed emPY/reAN/
    RINGS to/ the ROAR/ of an AN/gel ONset—/
    me RA/ther ALL/ that BO/wery LONE/liNESS,/
    the BROOKS/ of E/den MA/zily MUR/muRING,/   10
    and BLOOM/ proFUSE/ and CE/dar ARches/
    CHARM, as/ a WAN/derer OUT/ in Ocean,/
    where SOME/ reFUL/gent SUN/set of IN/diA/
    STREAMS o'er/ a RICH/ amBRO/sial O/cean ISLE,/
    and CRIM/son-HUED/ the STATE/ly PALM-woods/   15
    WHISper/ in O/dorous HEIGHTS/ of Even./
                            (Tennyson, "MILTON," 1863)

_____

*bisyllabic?

Strangely stiff, particularly for the smooth verse of Tennyson, this is nevertheless perfectly scannable, as well as regular in its

121

alternation of a pair of iambic pentameter and a pair of iambic tetrameter lines. Once again, however, the poem is the product of educated British longing for classical times and classical certainties: Tennyson explicitly declared "Milton" to be a poem written, not in English meter at all, but in the Greek measure known as Alcaic. There is no need, by this point, to discuss Tennyson's success or failure. What is perhaps most remarkable is not that, in 1863, he was still trying to do—and thought he had done—the impossible, but that in the last decade of the twentieth century there are poets still struggling in the same hopeless, senseless cause.

e.   GR-R-R/ there GO,/ my HEART'S/ abHORrence!/
          WAter/ YOUR damned/ FLOWer-/pots, DO!/
      IF hate/ KILLED men,/ BROther/ LAWrence,/
          GOD'S blood,/ WOULD not/ MINE/ kill YOU!/
      WHAT?/ your MYR/tle BUSH/ wants TRIMming?/   5
          OH,/ that ROSE/ has PRI/or CLAIMS—/
      NEEDS/ its LEA/den VASE/ filled BRIMming?/
          HELL/ dry YOU/ up WITH/ its FLAMES!/

      AT/ the MEAL/ we SIT/ toGEther:/
          SAL/ve TIB/i! I/ must HEAR/   10
      WISE/ talk OF/ the KIND/ of WEAther,/
          SORT/ of SEA/son, TIME/ of YEAR:/
      NOT/ a PLEN/teous CORK/-crop:/ SCARCEly
          DARE/ we HOPE/ oak-GALLS,/ i DOUBT:/
      WHAT'S/ the LA/tin NAME/ for PARsley?/   15
          WHAT'S/ the GREEK/ name FOR/ swine's
              SNOUT?/ . . .
                          (Robert Browning, "Soliloquy of the
                          Spanish Cloister," 1842: excerpt)

      _____

      *salve tibi = greetings; hello

Again, conventional scansion seems almost beside the point, here. This is clearly tetrameter. But each line of the poem contains seven or eight syllables, in no particular sequence, and many of the intended scansions can only be achieved by high-order violence to the English language. To proceed backwards,

122

for visual convenience: of the four final words quoted, three are likely candidates for linguistic stress, but "for," which receives metrical stress, is not one of them. In line fourteen, "OAK-gall" is a standard English compound, invariably accented on the first, not the last, syllable. In line eleven, standard Chaucerian Compromise prosody requires that "wise TALK" be accented, as just marked, with the second syllable stressed, but here the meter requires "WISE talk." The initial stress on "at," in line nine, is extremely odd, linguistically. "hell DRY," at the start of line eight, would be thus scanned, in traditional Chaucerian Compromise prosody; but here it needs to be scanned "HELL dry." At the start of line four, both traditional Chaucerian prosody and natural linguistic stress would produce "god's BLOOD"; Browning intends "GOD'S blood." Line three in traditional Chaucerian Compromise prosody would be marked "if HATE/ killed MEN"; here, it needs to be scanned "IF hate/ KILLED MEN"—or does it? Does Browning really care? *Can* he really care, given the facts just summarized?

f.   ah, DID/ you ONCE/ see SHEL/ley PLAIN,/
         and DID/ he STOP/ and SPEAK/ to YOU/
     and DID/ you SPEAK/ to HIM/ aGAIN?/
         how STRANGE/ it SEEMS/ and NEW!/

     but YOU/ were LI/ving BE/fore THAT,/   5
         and AL/so YOU/ are LI/ving AFter;/
     AND the/MEmory*/ i START/ed AT—/
         my START/ing MOVES/ your LAUGHter./

     i CROSSED/ a MOOR,/ with a NAME/ of its OWN/
         and a CER/tain USE/ in the WORLD/ no DOUBT,/   10
     yet a HAND'S/-breadth OF/ it SHINES/ aLONE/
         mid the BLANK/ miles ROUND/ aBOUT:/

     for THERE/ i PICKED/ up ON/ the HEAther/
         and THERE/ i PUT/ inSIDE/ my BREAST/
     a MOUL/ted FEA/ther, an EA/gle-FEAther!/   15
         WELL, i/ forGET/ the REST./
                     (Browning, "Memorabilia," 1855)

_____

*bisyllabic?

123

Browning uses four quatrains, rhyming A B A B, with the first three lines of each in tetrameter, and the fourth and last in trimeter. The replicative structure is both plain and tightly constructed. But the prosodic pattern is achieved only by a good deal of more or less severe violence to the language. There is no way to avoid the scansion marked for line five, which requires the linguistically impossible reversal of stress, "BEfore." Line eleven obliges us to give greater metrical stress to "of" than to "breadth," though "breadth" as the second half of a compound may help explain this. But the scansion of line twelve does considerable violence to the word "miles," as indeed we also find it difficult not to give metrical stress to "mid" at the start of the line. It is linguistically far more usual to stress the first syllable of "INside" than the second, as here. "inSIDE" is not impossible; it is, again, distinctly less likely. (And arguably Browning intended the scansion here to be "INside/ my BREAST".) Note too that the poet has, though not I think deliberately, given us something of a false signal by fashioning the prosody of the first stanza in emphatically regular fashion. This begins to break down only a bit, in stanza two, with its two feminine rhymes (plus the mangling of "before"). But six of the fifteen metrical feet in the third stanza are trisyllabic, indicating a significantly increased divergence from the regularity of stanza one—and mutually contradictory signals, as we have already noted, are part and parcel of the metrical developments we have been observing.

g.   'will SPRAWL*,/ NOW that/ the HEAT/ of DAY/ is
          BEST,/
     FLAT on/ his BEL/ly IN/ the PIT'S/ much MIRE,/
     with EL/bows WIDE,/ fists CLENCHED/ to
          PROP/ his CHIN./
     and, WHILE/ he KICKS/ both FEET/ IN the/
          cool SLUSH,/
     and FEELS/ aBOUT/ his SPINE/ small EFT/-things
          COURSE,/   5
     run IN/ and OUT/ each ARM,/ and MAKE/ him
          LAUGH:/
     and WHILE/ aBOVE/ his HEAD/ a
          POM/pion-PLANT,/

COATing/ the CAVE/-top AS/ a BROW/ its EYE,/
creeps DOWN/ to TOUCH/ and TICK/le HAIR/
   and BEARD,/
and NOW/ a FLOW/er DROPS/ with a BEE/ inSIDE,/   10
and NOW/ a FRUIT/ to SNAP/ at, CATCH/ and
   CRUNCH,—/
he LOOKS/ out O'ER/ you SEA/ which SUN/beams
   CROSS/
and RE/cross TILL/ they WEAVE/ a SPI/der-WEB/
(MEshes/ of FIRE,/ some GREAT/ fish BREAKS/ at
   TIMES)/
and tALKS/ to HIS/ own SELF,/ howE'ER/ he
   PLEASE,/   15
TOUching/ that O/ther, WHOM/ his DAM/ called GOD./
beCAUSE/ to TALK/ aBOUT/ him, VEX/es—HA,/
could HE/ but kNOW!/ and TIME/ to VEX/ is NOW,/
when TALK/ is SA/fer THAN/ in WIN/ter-TIME./
moreO/ver PROS/per AND/ miRAN/da SLEEP/   20
in CON/fiDENCE/ he DRUD/ges AT/ their TASK,/
and IT/ is GOOD/ to CHEAT/ the PAIR,/ and GIBE,/
LETting/ the RANK/ tongue BLOS/som IN/to
   SPEECH./

SE/teBOS,/ SE/teBOS,/ and SE/teBOS!/
THINKeth,/ *he dwelleth* i' the COLD/ of the
   MOON./   25

THINKeth/ he MADE/ it, WITH/ the SUN/ to
   MATCH,/
but NOT/ the STARS;/ the STARS/ came
   O/therWISE;/
ONly/ made CLOUDS, winds, ME/teors, SUCH/ as
   THAT:/
ALso/ this ISLE,/ what LIVES/ and GROWS/
   thereON,/
and SNA/ky SEA/ which ROUNDS/ and ENDS/ the
   SAME./   30

THINKeth,/ it CAME/ of BE/ing ILL/ at EASE:/
he HA/ted THAT/ he CAN/not CHANGE/ his
   COLD,/

nor CURE/ its ACHE./ 'hath SPIED/ an I/cy FISH/
that LONGED/ to 'SCAPE/ the ROCK/-stream
   WHERE/ she LIVED,/
and THAW/ herSELF withIN/ the LUKE/warm
   BRINE/   35
o' the LA/zy SEA/ her STREAM/ thrusts FAR/
   aMID,/
a CRYS/tal SPIKE/ 'twixt TWO/ warm WALLS/
   of WAVE;/
ONly,/ she E/ver SICK/ened, FOUND/
   rePULSE/
at the O/ther KIND/ of WA/ter, NOT/ her LIFE,/
(green-DENSE/ and DIM/-deLI/cious, BRED/ o'
   the SUN)/   40
flounced BACK/ from BLISS/ she WAS/ not BORN/
   to BREATHE,/
and IN/ her OLD/ bounds BU/ried HER/ desPAIR,/
HAting/ and LO/ving WARMTH/ aLIKE:/ so
   HE./ . . .

what, WHAT?/ a CUR/tain O'ER/ the WORLD/ at
   ONCE!/
CRICkets/ stop HIS/sing; NOT/ a BIRD/—or, YES,/   285
there SCUDS/ his RA/ven THAT/ has TOLD/ him
   ALL!/
IT was/ FOOL'S play,/ this PRAT/tling! HA!/ the
   WIND/
SHOULders/ the PIL/lared DUST,/ death's HOUSE/
   o' the MOVE,/
and FAST/ inVA/ding FIRES/ beGIN!/ white
   BLAZE —/
a TREE'S/ head SNAPS/—and THERE,/ there,
   THERE,/ there, THERE,/   290
his THUN/der FOL/lows! FOOL/ to GIBE/ at HIM!/
lo! LI/eth FLAT/ and LO/veth SE/teBOS!/
MAketh/ his TEETH/ meet THROUGH/ his
   UP/per LIP,/
will LET/ those QUAILS/ fly, WILL/ not EAT/ this
   MONTH/
one LIT/tle MESS/ of WHELKS,/ so HE/ may
   'SCAPE!/   295
           (Browning, ''Caliban upon Setebos,'' 1860: excerpts)

*perhaps *almost* bisyllabic?

Browning plainly cares enough about traditional Chaucerian Compromise prosody to at least preserve the *appearance* of metrical regularity and formality. But though it is technically correct to mark metrical feet, here, and there are a fair number of lines which are actually framed in traditional iambic pentameter, there are many more that push the working rules of traditional prosody over the edge. Line two hundred and ninety, e.g., so stretches the convention which allocates metrical stress to the second of two equally matched syllables that the convention becomes virtually meaningless. There is *no* stress distinction between the five iterations of "there," in linguistic reality: actually pronounced anything like the prosodic marking, here, the words would sound ludicrous. So large a difference between prosodic and linguistic stress, once again, marks a vital breakdown in the Chaucerian Compromise. The same is true of the twice iterated "what" at the start of line two hundred and eighty-four. And the poetic convention just discussed is also badly stretched at a number of other points—in lines three, six, fourteen, twenty-eight, thirty-six, forty, forty-one, two hundred and eighty-eight, and two hundred and eighty-nine. Line twenty-four cannot be turned into a five-stress line, counting by either traditional prosody or linguistic methods; the second foot of line twenty-five, similarly, cannot be definitively scanned either as "he DWELL/eth" or "HE dwelleth/". The natural linguistic reading of line eight is more like "COATing the CAVE-TOP as a BROW its EYE"—which I have not divided into metrical feet because, *tout court*, I'm not sure there really are any. Browning is careful to give nice syntactical support to the stress on "now" in line one: the word is chimed at us in lines ten, eleven, and eighteen. But there is no consistent correspondence between "He" and "Him," words used to represent the deity, and metrical stress. "Him" is metrically unstressed in line seventeen; "He" is metrically stressed in line eighteen. "He" is metrically unstressed in line thirty-two (twice), as is "His," but metrically stressed again in line forty-three. "His" and "Him" are both metrically unstressed in line two hundred and eighty-six; "His" is metrically unstressed in line two hundred and ninety-one, though the same line gives metrical stress to "Him."

We do not need to count trisyllabic feet, in the fifty-five lines reproduced here, to see how the Chaucerian Compromise has faded. Indeed, there are remarkably few trisyllabic feet, considering all the other irregularities. We are better off listening to the music of these lines, particularly to the exceedingly poor corre-spondence between the natural (linguistic) music and the required prosodic markings. The "tacit" metrical knowledge discussed by Halle and Keyser, in the epigraph to this book, here causes the average reader to have frequent and serious difficulty in distin-guishing metrical from unmetrical lines. Again, the social agree-ment underlying the Chaucerian Compromise had to have been badly shaken for a great poet to produce such lines. Caliban is concededly something of a monster; it would be in character for a monster to speak and think monstrously. But would a dramatic poet like Shakespeare, in whose time the Chaucerian Compro-mise flourished, have cast the words of such a character in prosody of this sort? Or John Milton, whose *Paradise Lost* features the direst of all Christian monsters?

h. in a COIGN/ of the CLIFF/ between LOW/land and
       HIGHland,/
    at the SEA/-down's EDGE/ between WIND/ward and
       LEE,/
  walled ROUND/ with ROCKS/ as an IN/land ISland,/
       the GHOST/ of a GAR/den FRONTS/ the SEA./
  a GIR/dle of BRUSH/wood and THORN/ enCLOses/   5
       the STEEP/ square SLOPE/ of the BLOS/somless
       BED/
  where the WEEDS/ that grew GREEN/ from the
       GRAVES/ of its ROses/
       NOW/ lie DEAD./ . . .

                  (Algernon Charles Swinburne, "A
                  Forsaken Garden," 1876: excerpt)

Swinburne clearly likes the shimmering length of a full anapestic line, made even longer by a feminine ending. But only two of the seven full-length lines, here, are in fact straight anapestic, and in the other five the two metrical patterns, anapestic and iambic, alternate in what should by now be a familiar fashion. That is, (a) there is no particular pattern to their alternation, and (b) the frequencies are pretty much balanced as between the two. There are eleven iambic feet in the five non-anapestic lines, and nine anapestic ones. In what prosodic measure can we say this stanza, and indeed the rest of the eighty-line poem to which it belongs, has been written? The poem is in a basic tetrameter, to be sure, with a final dimeter line—but tetrameter *what*? and dimeter *what*? And if we cannot, as in fact we cannot, stipulate a prosodic measure, are we not close to tetrameter as meaning not much more than four stresses per line? (Swinburne is almost insanely fond of alliteration, that bulwark of the Old English four-stress line.)

i. when the HOUNDS/ of SPRING/ are on WIN/ter's TRAces,/
       the MO/ther of MONTHS/ in MEA/dow or PLAIN/
       FILLS the/ SHAdows/ and WIN/dy PLAces
         with LISP/ of LEAVES/ and RIP/ple of RAIN;/
       and the BROWN/ bright NIGHT/ingale A/moROUS/   5
       is HALF/ asSUAGED/ for I/tyLUS,/
       for the THRA/cian SHIPS/ and the FO/reign FAces,/
       the TONGUE/less VI/gil and ALL/ the PAIN./ . . .
        (Swinburne, *Atalanta in Calydon*: "When the Hounds of
        Spring Are on Winter's Traces," 1865: excerpt)

Eight lines of tetrameter, if tetrameter is (as it appears to be) what this poem intends, make for a total of thirty-two metrical feet. It may seem as if there are more, but ten of those metrical feet, here, are trisyllabic. The effect is much like that of the first stanza from Swinburne, above. Prosodic certainty is so disrupted, indeed, that line five becomes difficult to scan. Natural linguistic stresses occur on "brown," "bright," and the first syllable of both "nightingale" and of "amorous." (The linguistic stress on "bright" is lighter and could well be eliminated.) This is obviously not the metrical pattern Swinburne intends, nor that he has emphatically signalled to us from the start. (It does not seem accidental that four of the ten trisyllabic feet occur in the first two lines: Swinburne is far too practiced a poet, and far too metrically conscious, not to know what he is doing in these matters). Do we then give metrical stress to the first word in the line, "And"? Though this would be perfectly possible, and permissible, the balance of this fifty-five-line poem has no fewer than eleven additional instances of lines beginning with "and," not one of which is metrically stressed. It therefore seems unlikely that the word ought to have metrical stress here. Further, the rhyme-word "amorous" is paired with "Itylus" in the very next line, and the metrical patterning makes that unmistakeably a double-stressed word: "ItylUS." By this process of elimination, we find ourselves assigning two metrical stresses to "Amo-ROUS" as well, and thus framing the required tetrameter. It is a perfectly acceptable scansion, but there are—once again—two striking reasons for the difficulty:

(1) the prosodic patterning of the poem as a whole is intrinsically indecipherable, nominally "anapestic" and nominally "iambic" feet alternating in no predictable fashion, and

(2) metrical stresses do not always match well with linguistic stresses.

17 / Whitman and Dickinson

a. Well, the lilt is all right: yes, right enough: but there's something anterior—more imperative. The first thing necessary is the thought—the rest may follow if it chooses—may play its part—but must not be too much sought after. The two things being equal I should prefer to have the lilt present with the idea, but if I got down my thought and the rhythm was not there I should not work to secure it. I am very deliberate—I take a good deal of trouble with words: yes, a good deal: but what I am after is the content and not the music of words. Perhaps the music happens—it does no harm: I do not go in search of it. Two centuries back or so much of the poetry passed from lip to lip—was oral: was literally made to be sung: then the lilt, the formal rhythm, may have been necessary. The case is now somewhat changed: now, when the poetic work in literature is more than nineteen-twentieths of it by print, the simply tonal aids are not so necessary, or, if necessary, have considerably shifted their character. . . . They talk about form: poetic form: this tradition for sculpture, that for painting, another for the written word: complying to the dicta of professors, pedagogues, stylists, grammarians. Well—a man can do that and be crowned: then he can not do it and take his chances. . . . I have never looked for finish—never fooled with technique more than enough to provide for simply getting through: after that I would not give a twist of my chair for all the rest. . . . People get accustomed to a certain order of traditions, forms: they think these a part of nature, or nature itself—that they are never to be displaced, are eternal: they will not be easily shaken out of their conviction even when they know all their

131

vitality has departed . . . There are times when the house cannot be patched any more but *asks to be taken down*.
(Walt Whitman to Horace Traubel, 16 May 1888, 8 Feb. 1889, 12 Nov. 1888, 16 Mar. 1889

b. i CELebrate mySELF, and SING mySELF,
and what I asSUME YOU shall asSUME,
for EVEry ATom beLONGing to ME as GOOD
    beLONGS to YOU.

i LOAF and inVITE my SOUL,
i LEAN and LOAF at my EASE obSERVing a
    SPEAR of SUMmer GRASS.   5

my TONGUE, EVEry ATom of my BLOOD,
    FORMED from this SOIL, this AIR,
born HERE of PArents born HERE from PArents the
    SAME, and THEIR
    PArents the SAME,
I, now THIRty SEVen years OLD in PERfect HEALTH
    beGIN,
HOPing to CEASE not till DEATH.

CREEDS and SCHOOLS in aBEYance,   10
reTIRing BACK a WHILE sufFICED at WHAT they
    ARE, but NEver forGOTten,
i HARbor for GOOD or BAD, i perMIT to SPEAK at
    EVEry HAzard,
NAture withOUT CHECK WITH oRIginal
    ENergy.
        (Walt Whitman, "Song of Myself": Poem 1, 1855)

It is not that this poetry *cannot* be scanned, but rather that it *should not* be scanned. The correspondence between Whitman's prosody and the natural linguistic movement of the language is absolute—and the linguistic standard is the only one to be used. There being a close relationship between Chaucerian Compromise verse at its best and the natural linguistic movement of the language, it is inevitable that much of Whitman's "free verse" *could* be scanned. Much—but not all: the resemblance of this prosody to that of Swinburne and Browning, in particular, is historically understandable. And yet too much should not be made of the fact. Consider what would happen if we took the prosody above indicated and, keeping stresses and stresses exactly as they are marked, tried to turn them into metrical stresses and unstresses, dividing the lines, in the process, into metrical feet:

i CEL/ebrate mySELF,/ and SING/ mySELF,/
and what I/ asSUME/ YOU shall/ asSUME,/
for EVE/ry AT/om beLONG/ing to ME/ as GOOD/
beLONGS/ to YOU./

i LOAF/ and inVITE/ my SOUL,/
i LEAN/ and LOAF/ at my EASE/ obSERV/ing a
    SPEAR/ of SUM/mer GRASS./   5

my TONGUE,/ EVEry/ ATom/ of my BLOOD,/ FORMED
    from/ this SOIL,/ this AIR,/
born HERE/ of PA/rents born HERE/ from PA/rents
    the SAME,/ and THEIR/ PArents/ the SAME,/
I, now/ THIRty/ SEVen/ years OLD/ in PER/fect
    HEALTH/ beGIN,/
HOPing/ to CEASE/ not till DEATH./

CREEDS/ and SCHOOLS/ in abEYance,/   10
reTIR/ing BACK/ a WHILE/ sufFICED/ at WHAT/
    they ARE,/ but NE/ver forGOTten,/
i HAR/bor for GOOD/ or BAD,/ i perMIT/ to
    SPEAK/ at EVE/ry HAzard,/
NAture/ withOUT/ CHECK/ WITH o/RI/ginal ENergy./

The second foot of line one has three unstressed syllables, a situation which Chaucerian Compromise prosody would easily rectify by giving metrical stress to the third syllable in "CELe-BRATE." The line would then become perfect iambic pentameter, would acquire exactly the "lilt" that Whitman's critics missed in his verse and wished they could find there. It would also cease to have any resemblance to Whitman's true poetic voice.

Line two would then be iambic tetrameter—the first and third feet irregular, but no more so than in Browning and Swinburne.

Line three would then be an almost regular iambic heptameter—an odd metrical choice, had Whitman in fact made it, but hardly revolutionary.

Line four would then be an almost regular iambic trimeter.

Line five would then be a mildly irregular iambic heptameter (the sequencing plainly growing odder and odder).

Line six would then be a very strange heptameter, three of its seven feet trochaic, one trisyllabic (i.e., nominally dactylic), and three regular iambic. What does one label such a line?

Line seven would then be octameter, with two trisyllabic feet and one trochaic—yet another very strange line.

Line eight would then be heptameter, with the first three feet trochaic.

Line nine would then be trimeter, with a reversed or trochaic first foot and a trisyllabic or anapestic third one—i.e., trimeter to be sure, but trimeter *what*?

Line ten would then be trimeter too, again with a trisyllabic final foot, but with a monosyllabic first foot. Again, trimeter *what*?

Line eleven would then be an almost regular octameter, with the final foot both trisyllabic and having a feminine ending.

Line twelve would then be mildly irregular heptameter (two trisyllabic feet).

And line thirteen would then be irregular hexameter, the first foot reversed, the third foot monosyllabic, the fourth and fifth feet reversed, and the sixth foot with a double feminine ending.

The exercise is not only totally conditional—as I have tried to indicate with a string of "would then be" phrases—but clearly erroneous. We know this is not what Whitman was up to. But the exercise is not a futile one, for it helps to underline how small a distance Whitman in fact had to travel, in order to escape, as it were, from the gravitational pull of the Chaucerian Compromise.

c. when i HEARD the LEARN'D asTROnomer,
    when the PROOFS, the FIgures, were RANGED in
        COlumns beFORE me,

when i was SHOWN the CHARTS and DIagrams,
    to ADD, diVIDE, and MEAsure them,
when I SITting HEARD the asTROnomer WHERE he
    LECtured with MUCH apPLAUSE in the
    LECture-room,
how SOON unacCOUNtable i became TIRED and SICK,   5
till RISing and GLIDing OUT i WANDER'D OFF by
    mySELF,
in the MYstical MOIST NIGHT-AIR, and from TIME to
    TIME,
look'd UP in PERfect SIlence at the STARS.
    (Whitman, "When I Heard the Learn'd Astronomer," 1865)

Much like the first passage quoted from Whitman, above, this
also features usages that might well be mistaken for the prosodic
apostrophe: "learn'd," "wander'd." Since the second instance,
"wander'd," would have precisely the same pronunciation and
syllable count with or without the apostrophe, it seems pretty
clearly to be nothing more than orthographical habit. Precisely
what Whitman intended by "learn'd," however, is less readily
determinable, since (a) in its adjectival form "learned" *is* bisyllabic, (b) in its verb form it is monosyllabic, and (c) it is the
adjectival form that is here employed. Did Whitman intend it to
be monosyllabic, here? Or is this too simply orthographical habit?
Without making an exhaustive orthographical check of his poetry, it would appear that while almost all the usages which might
be construed as the prosodic apostrophe are in truth mere spelling
tics ("scattr'd, appear'd, crouch'd"), "learn'd" does in fact
reflect a pronunciation choice rather than a prosodic one. In part
three of "Song of Myself," e.g., he writes "learn'd and unlearn'd
feel that it is so." Which makes perfectly good sense, for we are
all entitled to our personal quibbles. But there is no need to
elevate Whitman's to Chaucerian Compromise status.

d.

    1
when LIlacs LAST in the DOORyard BLOOM'D,
and the GREAT STAR EARLY DROOP'D in the
    WEStern SKY in the NIGHT,

135

i MOURN'D, and YET shall MOURN with
Ever-reTURNing SPRING.

Ever reTURNing SPRING, TRInity SURE to ME you
BRING,
LIlac BLOOMing peRENnial and DROOPing STAR
in the WEST,   5
and THOUGHT of HIM i LOVE.

2
o POWerful WEStern FALLing STAR!
o SHADES of NIGHT—o MOOdy, TEARful NIGHT!
o GREAT STAR disapPEAR'D—o the BLACK
MURK that HIDES the STAR!
o CRUEL HANDS that HOLD me POWerless—o
HELPless SOUL of ME!   10
o HARSH surROUNDing CLOUD that WILL not
FREE my SOUL. . . .

(Whitman, "When Lilacs Last in the
Dooryard Bloom'd," 1865–66: excerpt)

We do not know precisely how Whitman meant these lines to be
read (*not* scanned: that is obvious from line two alone). But the
reading just marked is a reasonable facsimile, though surely one
that different readers will change, and also different times. As
thus marked, how like the prosody of Swinburne and Browning
this is—and yet at the same time how utterly unlike.

e.   some THINGS/ that FLY/ there BE —/
          BIRDS—hours —/ the BUM/bleBEE —/
          of THESE/ no E/leGY./

          some THINGS/ that STAY/ there BE —/
          GRIEF—hills —/ eTER/niTY —/   5
          nor THIS/ beHOO/veth ME./

          there ARE/ that REST/ing, RISE./
          can I/ exPOUND/ the SKIES?/
          how STILL/ the RID/dle LIES!/
          (Emily Dickinson, Poem 89, 1859?)

136

The psychological rule of conservation of energy ensures, in matters of artistic creativity, that anyone who revolutionizes one aspect of his or her art will probably more or less tamely follow the leader in most other aspects. A primary corollary of the rule is that no one can be a pioneer in everything. Emily Dickinson's approach to metaphor and diction, to tone and poetic flow, was about as revolutionary as could be. Accordingly, her approach to meter and form was inevitably a great deal more conventional, especially at the start of her career.

The principle of replicative form would seem to require that lines two and five, each of which contain four natural linguistic stresses, should be governed by the Chaucerian Compromise and its conventions, as the rest of the poem appears to be.

f. HOW ma/ny TIMES/ these LOW/ feet STAGgered —/
    ONly/ the SOL/dered MOUTH/ can TELL —/
    TRY—can/ you STIR/ the AW/ful RIvet —/
    TRY—can/ you LIFT/ the HASPS/ of STEEL!/

    STROKE the/ cool FORE/head—HOT/ so OFten —/   5
    LIFT—if/ you CARE —/ the LIST/less HAIR —/
    HANdle/ the A/daMAN/tine FINgers/
    NEver/ a THIM/ble—MORE —/ shall WEAR —/

    BUZZ the/ dull FLIES/ on the CHAM/ber WINdow —
    BRAVE—shines/ the SUN/ through the FRECK/led
        PANE —/   10
    FEARless —/ the COB/web SWINGS/ from the
        CEILing —/
    INdo/lent HOUSE/wife—in DAI/sies—LAIN!/
                        (Dickinson, Poem 187, 1860?)

The rhyming is not only less insistent—the first Dickinson poem, above, rhymes A A A A A A B B B—but deliberately imperfect. "Tell" and "steel" make about as weak a claim to rhyming as a poet can put forward. Further, the unrhymed feminine endings of lines one, three, five, seven, nine, and eleven are presented as if an extra syllable added to each line is somehow a fact of replicative importance—as indeed it is, but not in traditional Chaucerian Compromise terms. Finally, each line of the third and last stanza

137

contains a trisyllabic foot. None of these are matters of crucial importance or weight; taken together, they seem to point toward at least the possibility of a loosening concern for traditional poetic techniques, including prosodic ones.

g. i TASTE/ a LI/quor NE/ver BREWED —/
    from TAN/kards SCOOPED/ in PEARL —/
    not ALL/ the FRANK/fort BERries/
    yield SUCH/ an AL/coHOL!/

    iNE/briATE/ of AIR —/ am I —/   5
    and DE/bauCHEE/ of DEW —/
    REELing/ through END/less SUM/mer DAYS —/
    from INNS/ of MOL/ten BLUE —/

    when "LAND/lords" TURN/ the DRUN/ken BEE
    OUT of/ the FOX/glove's DOOR —/   10
    when BUT/terFLIES/—reNOUNCE/ their "DRAM" —/
    I shall/ but DRINK/ the MORE!/

    till SE/raphs SWING/ their SNO/wy HATS —/
    and SAINTS —/ to WIN/dows RUN —/
    to SEE/ the LIT/tle TIPpler/   15
    from MAN/zaNIL/la COME!/
                            (Dickinson, Poem 214, 1860–61?)

Rhyming is again irregular ("pearl" and "alcohol," "run" and "come," as well as "dew" and "blue"—if that is for Dickinson "dew" contained a [y] glide after the initial [d]). There is a kind of replicative pattern, here, with the first and fourth stanzas starting with an iambic tetrameter line and proceeding to three consecutive trimeter lines, while the two middle stanzas alternate tetrameter and trimeter. But though it can be understood to emerge from the Chaucerian Compromise warehouse, the pattern is anything but traditional. There are no trisyllabic feet, but the two feminine endings (lines three and fifteen) are in no way patterned: they occur willy-nilly.

h. to MAKE/ a PRAI/rie it TAKES/ a CLO/ver *and one bee*,
    one clover, and a bee,

138

and RE/veRY.
the RE/veRY/ aLONE/ will DO/
if BEES/ are FEW./   5
(Dickinson, Poem 1755, 1885?)

A quarter of a century later, toward the end of her life, Dickinson
has clearly begun to cast off even her time's relatively free
prosodic normalcy. Line one is perhaps to be scanned, at the
end, "AND/ one BEE," but alternative scansions seem just as
possible: "and ONE bee"? "and one BEE"? "AND/ one BEE/
"? The scansion of line one will then determine the scansion of
line two, which otherwise will flap between a linguistically accented dimeter and a traditionally accented trimeter. There is no
respect whatever paid to replicative form: were it not for the
wryly effective rhyming, it might be arguable that Dickinson had
cast off the Chaucerian Compromise (though it does not appear
to me that she ever took that step). Lines three and four may well
be meant to be scanned "and REvery./ // the RE/very aLONE/
will DO." It is even possible that "revery" should be considered
metrically bisyllabic. In sum, the sorts and degrees of irregularity, here, clearly align Dickinson with the best poets of her time,
in terms of her relationship to traditional prosody and technique.

18 / *Gerard Manley Hopkins*

a.   the WORLD/ is CHARGED/ WITH the/ GRANdeur/ of
      GOD./
        it WILL/ flame OUT,/ like SHIN/ing FROM/ shook
          FOIL;/
        it GA/thers to a GREAT/ness, LIKE/ the OOZE/
          of OIL/
      CRUSHED. why/ do MEN/ then NOW/ not RECK/
        his ROD?/
      GEne/RAtions/ have TROD,/ have TROD,/ have
        TROD;/   5
        and ALL/ is SEARED/ with TRADE;/ bleared,
          SMEARED/ with TOIL;/
        and WEARS/ man's SMUDGE/ and SHARES/
          man's SMELL:/ the SOIL/
      is BARE/ now, NOR/ can FOOT/ feel, BE/ing SHOD./

      AND for/ all THIS,/ NAture/ is NE/ver SPENT;/
        there LIVES/ the DEAR/est FRESH/ness
          DEEP/ down THINGS;/   10
      and THOUGH/ the LAST/ lights OFF/ the BLACK/ west
        WENT/
        oh MOR/ning AT/ the BROWN/ brink EAST/ward,
          SPRINGS —/
      beCAUSE/ the HO/ly GHOST/ Over/ the BENT/
        world BROODS/ with WARM/ BREAST and/
        with AH!/ bright WINGS./
          (Gerard Manley Hopkins, "God's Grandeur," 1877)

Hopkins noted that this poem was to be read "slowly, strongly marking the rhythms and fetching out the syllables"; he also declared that the prosody of the poem as a whole was "standard rhythm [i.e., Chaucerian Compromise prosody] counter-pointed"—and see the prose excerpt, below, for what Hopkins meant by "counterpointed." The scansion of line one, and that of the first two metrical feet of line five, has been marked by the poet. The scansion of line four follows Hopkins' instructions, though it does not easily follow the natural linguistic rhythms of the language. Even the ancient prosodic convention which stipulates that two syllables of equal stress within a foot give metrical precedence to the second, to preserve the basic iambic metric, is barely sufficient to keep "bleared, SMEARED," in line six, from being a spondee. A slow reading, as Hopkins requests, coupled with a clear caesura after "bleared," makes it extremely difficult to keep from stressing the first word quite as strongly as the second.

This is a poem of exceedingly heavy, even ponderous accent, carrying onomatopoeia about as far as it can go. "have TROD,/ have TROD,/ have TROD," thuds—and is meant to thud—in the ear like the tramping beat of long lines of slogging boots. The effect of heavy accent is reinforced by equally heavy and insistent alliteration: there is not a line without significant alliterative coupling (perhaps at its weakest in line thirteen, where Hopkins uses approximations rather than direct alliterations). The significance of conjoined heavy accenting and heavy alliteration hardly needs underlining—and indeed Hopkins, as shall see, was perfectly well aware of Old English prosody. The reversed feet, too, are not placed in more or less standard positions within the line, but wherever Hopkins happens to want them: feet three and four, in line one, foot three in line fourteen, and arguably also, though not so marked here, in feet one and two of line two and any of the first three feet of line four. There are no trisyllabic feet, though the second foot of line three has an unusually large number of metrically unstressed syllables, namely, three.

b.   i CAUGHT/ this MOR/ning MOR/ning's MI/nion,
          KING-/
       dom of DAY/light's DAU/phin, DAP/ple-dawn-
       drawn FAL/con, in his RIDing/

of the ROL/ling level UN/derNEATH/ him
  steady AIR,/ and STRIding/
HIGH there,/ how he RUNG/ upon the REIN/ of a
  WIM/pling WING/
in his EC/staSY!/ then OFF, off FORTH/ on
  SWING,/   5
  as a SKATE'S/ heel sweeps SMOOTH/ on a
  BOW/-bend: the HURL/ and GLIDing/
  reBUFFED/ the BIG/ WIND. my/ HEART in/
  HIding/
STIRRED for/ a BIRD, —/ the aCHIEVE/ of, the
  MAS/tery of the THING!/

brute BEAU/ty and VA/lour and ACT,/ oh, AIR,/
  pride, PLUME, here
  BUCkle!/ and the FIRE/ that BREAKS/ from
  thee THEN,/ a BILlion/   10
TIMES told/ LOVElier/ more DANgerous,/ O my/
  chevaLIER!/

no WON/der of it: SHEER/ PLOD makes/ PLOUGH
  down/ SILlion/
SHINE, and/ BLUE-bleak/ EMbers,/ AH/ my DEAR,/
  fall, GALL/ themSELVES,/ and GASH/
  GOLD-ver/MILlion./
                    (Hopkins, "The Windhover," 1877)

Hopkins has once again marked many of the metrical accents—
lines one, two and fourteen in their entirety, feet two through five
of line three, and a number of "outriding" (that is, prosodically
neutral) feet throughout. But it is clear that to preserve Chaucerian Compromise standards, here, we are pretty much obliged to
stand on our heads. Some of the lines fall with relative ease into
traditional metrical patterns. But lines two and three have a total
of sixteen syllables each, line six has fifteen, line eight has
fourteen, and line nine has thirteen: on the most elementary of
levels, it is virtually impossible to have an iambic pentameter line

with that many feet, especially when the poet is as fond of heavily stressed accents as is Hopkins, here as elsewhere. Perhaps it is the native conservatism of the British as opposed to the American mind; perhaps it has a connection with Hopkins' deep religious convictions. But whatever the reason, unlike Walt Whitman he was unable fully to let go of prosodic standards it was quite obvious that he had largely rejected. As the prose excerpt immediately below reveals, in this sense it is Hopkins who is quite prepared to stand (and most uncomfortably) on his head, in order to keep his verse within the traditional metrical fold. It is also plain that, like many dedicated experimenters and proselytizers, he takes highly personal views, often highly exaggerated, of commonly understood matters.

c. [These poems] are written some in Running Rhythm, the common rhythm in English use, some in Sprung Rhythm, and some in a mixture of the two. And those in the common rhythm are some counterpointed, some not.

Common English rhythm, called Running Rhythm above, is measured by feet of either two or three syllables and (putting aside the imperfect feet at the beginning and end of lines and also some unusual measures, in which feet seem to be paired together and double or composite feet arise) never more or less.

Every foot has one principal stress or accent, and this or the syllable it falls on may be called the Stress of the foot and the other part, the one or two unaccented syllables, the Slack. Feet (and the rhythms made out of them) in which the stress comes first are called Falling Feet and Falling Rhythms, feet and rhythm in which the slack comes first are called Rising Feet and Rhythms, and if the stress is between the two slacks there will be Rocking Feet and Rhythms. These distinctions are real and true to nature; but for purposes of scanning it is a great convenience to follow the example of music and take the stress always first, as the accent or the chief accent of music always comes first in a musical bar. If this is done there will be in common English verse only two possible feet—the so-called accentual Trochee and Dactyl, and correspondingly only two possible uniform rhythms, the so-called Trochaic and Dactylic. But they may be mixed and then what the Greeks called a Logaeodic* Rhythm arises. These are the facts and according to these the scanning of ordinary regularly-written English verse is very simple indeed and to bring in other principles is here unnecessary.

But because verse written strictly in these feet and by these principles will becomes same and tame the poets have brought in licences and departures from rule to give variety, and especially where the natural rhythm is rising, as in the common ten-syllable or five-foot verse, rhymed or blank. These irregularities are chiefly Reversed Feet and Reversed or Counterpoint Rhythm, which two things are two steps or degrees of licence in the same kind. By a reversed foot I mean the putting the stress where, to judge by the rest of the measure, the slack should be and the slack where the stress, and this is done freely at the beginning of a line and, in the course of a line, after a pause; only scarcely ever in the second foot or place and never in the last, unless when the poet designs some extraordinary effect; for those places are characteristic and sensitive and cannot well be touched. But the reversal of the first foot and of some middle foot after a strong pause is a thing so natural that our poets have generally done it, from Chaucer down, without remark and it commonly passes unnoticed and cannot be said to amount to a formal change of rhythm, but rather is that irregularity which all natural growth and motion shews. If however the reversal is repeated in two feet running, especially so as to include the sensitive second foot, it must be due either to great want of ear or else is a calculated effect, the superinducing or *mounting* of a new rhythm upon the old; and since the new or mounted rhythm is actually heard and at the same time the mind naturally supplies the natural or standard foregoing rhythm, for we do not forget what the rhythm is that by rights we should be hearing, two rhythms are in some manner running at once and we have something answerable to counterpoint in music . . . Of this kind of music Milton is the great master and the choruses of *Samson Agonistes* are written throughout in it—but with the disadvantage that he does not let the reader clearly know what the ground-rhythm is meant to be and so they have struck most readers as merely irregular. And in fact if you counterpoint throughout, since one only of the counter rhythms is actually heard, the other is really destroyed or cannot come to exist, and what is written is one rhythm only and probably Sprung Rhythm, of which I now speak.

Sprung Rhythm, as used in [these poems], is measured by feet of from one to four syllables, regularly, and for particular effects any number of weak or slack syllables may be used. It has one stress, which falls on the only syllable, if there is only one, or, if there are more, then scanning as above, on the first, and so gives rise to four sorts of feet, a monosyllable and the so-called accentual Trochee, Dactyl, and the First Paeon†. And there will be four corresponding natural rhythms; but nominally the feet are mixed and any one may follow any other. And hence Sprung Rhythm differs from Running Rhythm in having only one nominal rhythm, a mixed or "logaoedic"* one, instead of three, but on the other hand in having twice the flexibility of foot, so that any two stresses may either follow one another running or be divided by one, two, or three slack syllables. But strict Sprung Rhythm cannot be counterpointed. . . .

Sprung Rhythm is the most natural of things. For (1) it is the rhythm of common speech and of written prose, when rhythm is perceived in them. (2) It is the rhythm of all but the most monotonously regular music, so that in the words of choruses and refrains and in songs written closely to music it arises. (3) It is found in nursery rhymes, weather saws, and so on; because, however these may have once been made in running rhythm, the terminations having dropped off by the change of language, the stresses come together and so the rhythm is sprung. (4) It arises in common verse when reversed or counterpointed, for the same reason.

But nevertheless in spite of all this and though Greek and Latin lyric verse, which is well known, and the Old English verse seen in "Pierce Ploughman" are in sprung rhythm, it has in fact ceased to be used since the Elizabethan age . . . For perhaps there was not, down to our days, a single, even short, poem in English in which sprung rhythm is employed—not for single effects or in fixed places—but as the governing principle of the scansion. I say this because the contrary has been asserted: if it is otherwise the poems should be cited.

(Hopkins, "Author's Preface," ca. 1883)

---

*logaoedic = mixed iambs, dactyls, trochees, and anapests
†First Paeon = a long followed by three consecutive shorts

This is not the place for a full discussion either of Hopkins' principles or of the inconsistencies and errors he makes in this theoretical presentation. One key assertion in the third paragraph should however be underlined: if we will only accent verse as we accent music, Hopkins notes with disarming blandness, namely on the first syllable in the line, we will always and exclusively have either trochaic or dactylic meter as the "only two possible feet" of English poetry. "These are the facts," he then asserts—going on, in the very next paragraph, to talk of the "common ten-syllable or five-foot verse, rhymed or blank," in which "the natural rhythm is rising." That "Common" measure is, though he carefully avoids the terms, also known as iambic pentameter. How it comes to be "common" when there are "in common English verse only two possible feet—the so-called accentual Trochee and Dactyl," Hopkins does not tell us.

d.   GLOry/ BE to/ GOD for/ DAPpled/ THINGS* —/
         for SKIES/ of COUP/le-CO/lour as a BRIN/ded
            COW;/
                  for ROSE/-moles ALL/ in STIP/ple
            upon TROUT/ that SWIM;/

      fresh-FIRE coal/ CHESTnut /FALLS;/ FINches/
            WINGS;/
      LANDscape/ PLOTted and/ PIECED—fold,/
         FALlow/ and PLOUGH;/   5
                  and ALL/ TRADES, their/ GEAR and/
            TACkle/ and TRIM./
      ALL things/ COUNter,/ oRI/ginal, SPARE,/
         STRANGE;/
         whatE/ver is FIC/kle, FREC/kled (WHO/ knows
            HOW?)
                  with swift, slow; sweet, sour;
                     addazzle, dim;
      he FA/thers FORTH,/ whose BEAU/ty is PAST/
         CHANGE:/   10
                  PRAISE/ HIM./
                  (Hopkins, "Pied Beauty," 1877)

   ────────────

   *Hopkins insisted that "dappled things"
   constituted two monosyllables, both stressed

146

Hopkins calls this "sprung paeonic rhythm," but I'm afraid that, as his scansion of "dappled" as a monosyllable shows, he is apt to be more than eccentric: this is plain wrong. I have tried to mark the scansion as, in his Preface, above, he indicates he wants it to be understood, but it does not always work. The English language keeps trying to swing up into iambic (that is, rising rather than falling), as in line one after the first two concededly trochaic (falling) feet: "to GOD/ for DAP/pled THINGS" is the natural reading. Further, the line has only nine syllables—and a trochee, like an iamb, consists of two syllables, making a total of ten distinctly desirable. Line four creates the same problem. And line nine, once again with a total of nine syllables, completely defeats me. On what consistent principle one can find five stresses in this line I do not know. The stresses in the first two feet of line six are, again, Hopkins' markings.

But would it not be more useful, as well as more accurate, to simply observe the stresses of verse like this, and not worry about the foot divisions? I feel confident that it would. Hopkins was of course even more confident that it would not—and one must defer to him. But for illustrative purposes, let me set out the next poem, a sprung rhythm sonnet that has six stresses per line, in the same manner used for Whitman's poetry, above.

e. NOT, i'll NOT, carrion COMfort, desPAIR, not FEAST
        on THEE;
    not unTWIST—SLACK they may BE—these LAST
        STRANDS of MAN
    IN me OR*, most WEAry, cry i CAN no MORE. i CAN;
    can SOMEthing, HOPE, wish DAY come, not CHOOSE
        NOT to BE.
    but AH, but O thou TERrible, WHY wouldst thou
        RUDE on ME   5
    thy WRING-world RIGHT foot ROCK? lay a
        LIonlimb aGAINST me? SCAN
    with DARKsome deVOUring EYES my BRUIsed*
        bones? and FAN,
    o in TURNS of TEMpest, me HEAPED there;
        me FRANtic to aVOID thee and FLEE?

147

WHY? that my CHAFF might FLY; my GRAIN
    lie, SHEER and CLEAR.
nay in ALL that TOIL, that COIL, since (SEEMS) i
    KISSED the ROD,   10
HAND rather, my HEART lo! lapped STRENGTH,
    stole JOY, would LAUGH, CHEER.
cheer WHOM though? the HEro whose
    HEAven-handling FLUNG me, FOOT TROD*
me? or ME that FOUGHT him? o which ONE? is it
    EACH one? that NIGHT, that YEAR
of NOW done DARKness i WRETCH lay WRESTling
    with (my GOD!) my GOD.

                           (Hopkins, Carrion Comfort,'' 1885)

---

*as marked by Hopkins

Consider line eight. If marked in metrical feet, it would look like this:

    o in TURNS/ of TEM/pest me HEAPED/ there;
    me FRAN/tic to aVOID/ thee and FLEE?/

Four of the six feet would be trisyllabic (anapestic), one would be bisyllabic (iambic), and one would have three unstressed syllables preceding the stressed syllable, which is not a standard Chaucerian Compromise meter (the Greeks would have called it a Fourth Paeonic). If we call the line hexameter, we revert to a familiar question: hexameter *what*? There are eighteen syllables in the line; there are fifteen in lines six and twelve. Given, too, Hopkins' fondness for stress-fractured syntax, for ancient and odd words, and for combinations like "wring-world," do we in fact gain anything by trying, at all costs, to pretend that this is simple, ordinary Chaucerian Compromise verse, just a little diddled here and fiddled there? The blunt truth, though as I have said Hopkins would not admit it, is that this is not Chaucerian Compromise verse at all.

148

The fact that Hopkins' poetry was not widely known before the publication, in 1918, of the first collection of his work—an edition of 1500 copies that did not, strikingly, sell out until 1930—is plainly *not* the causative factor in the essentially uninterrupted continuity of British prosody. British poetry was no more ready for Hopkins, in 1930, than it had been forty years earlier. The poems of section 19, "Edwardian England," clearly demonstrate the inability of British poetry to deal with the increasing instabilities and weaknesses of every aspect of traditional verse-making, just as the poems in the sections 20 and 21, "Frost, Pound, Eliot, Willams," and "Ten 20th-century American poets," clearly demonstrate how flexibly, powerfully, and excitingly adjustments of every sort were being made by Americans at home and abroad.

19 / *Edwardian England*

a.   ONly/ a MAN/ harrowing CLODS/
         in a SLOW/ silent WALK
with an OLD/ horse that STUM/bles and NODS/
         half aSLEEP/ as they STALK.

ONly/ thin SMOKE/ without FLAME/   5
         from the HEAPS/ of couch-GRASS;/
yet THIS/ will go ON/ward the SAME/
         though DY/nasties PASS./

YONder/ a MAID/ and her WIGHT/
         come WHIS/pering BY:/   10
war's AN/nals will CLOUD/ into NIGHT/
         ere THEIR/ story DIE./
                                  (Thomas Hardy, "In Time of
                                  'The Breaking of Nations'," 1915)

Although clearly Chaucerian Compromise poetry, this is as irregular as anything written by Swinburne or Browning. (It is also
much less flowing.) In stanza one, e.g., only the second foot of
line one, "a MAN," is in regular iambic meter. In stanza two,
only three of the ten metrical feet are regular; in stanza three
there are five (the highest total of all). Overall, accordingly, less
than a third of the poem's metrical feet are regular. Though still
at least nominally Chaucerian Compromise poetry, it is metrically
distinctly marginal.

150

b.   he STOOD,/ and HEARD/ the STEEple/
           SPRINkle/ the QUAR/ters ON/ the MOR/ning
           TOWN./
       one, TWO,/ three, FOUR,/ to MAR/ket-PLACE/ and
           PEOple/
       it TOSSED/ them DOWN./

       strapped, NOOSED,/ NIGHing/ his HOUR,/   5
           he STOOD/ and COUN/ted THEM and
           CURSED/ his LUCK;/
       and THEN/ the CLOCK/ colLEC/ted IN/ the TOwer/
           its STRENGTH,/ and STRUCK./
                 (A.E. Housman, "Eight O'clock," 1922)

More comfortably Chaucerian Compromise poetry, this still
strains at the bit. The distance between natural linguistic and
marked metrical movement in line three, e.g., is enormous; no
native speaker of English could keep from giving this line seven
full linguistic stresses: "ONE TWO THREE FOUR, to MARket-
PLACE and PEOPle." To force line five, similarly, into trimeter,
requires that we ignore the plainly imperative linguistic stress on
"strapped."

c.   but WERE/ i THOU,/ o Ocean,/
           i WOULD/ not CHAFE/ and FRET/
       as THOU,/ beCAUSE/ a LImit/
           to THY/ deSIRES/ is SET./

       I would/ be BLUE,/ and GENtle,/   5
           PAtient,/ and CALM,/ and SEE/
       if my SMI/les* MIGHT/ not TEMPT her,
           my LOVE,/ to COME/ to ME./

       i'd MAKE/ my DEPTHS/ transPArent,/
           and STILL,/ that SHE/ should LEAN/   10
       O'ER the/ boat's EDGE/ to PONder/
           the SIGHTS/ that SWAM/ beTWEEN./

       I would/ comMAND/ strange CREAtures,/
           OF bright/ HUE and/ quick FIN,/

<pre>
      to STIR/ the WA/ter NEAR her,/   15
      and TEMPT/ her BARE/ arm IN./

      i'd TEACH/ her SPEND/ the SUMmer
      with ME:/ and I/ can TELL,/
      that, WERE/ i THOU,/ o Ocean,/
      my LOVE/ should LOVE/ me WELL./   20

      but ON/ the MAD/ cloud SCUDded,/
      the BREEZE/ it BLEW/ so STIFF;/
      AND the/ sad O/cean BELlowed,/
      and POUN/ded AT/ the CLIFF./
            (Robert Bridges, "A Cloud," ca. 1890)
</pre>

*a meter-forced bisyllable?

More typically trivial, because written by a distinctly lesser poet, this is pretty much what Edwardian poetry, alas, is all about, both prosodically and in other ways.

<pre>
d.   I am/ the LAND/ of their FAthers./
      in ME/ the VIR/tue STAYS./
      I will/ bring BACK/ my CHILdren,/
      AFt/er CER/tain DAYS./

      UNder/ their FEET/ in the GRASses/   5
      my CLING/ing MA/gic RUNS./
      THEY shall/ reTURN/ as STRANgers./
      THEY shall/ reMAIN/ as SONS./

      Over/ their HEADS/ in the BRANches/
      of their NEW/-bought, AN/cient TREES,/   10
      i WEAVE/ an IN/canTAtion/
      and DRAW/ them TO/ my KNEES./

      SCENT/ of SMOKE/ in the EVEning,/
      SMELL/ of RAIN/ in the NIGHT—/
      the HOURS,/ the DAYS/ and the SEAsons,/   15
      ORder/ their SOULS/ aRIGHT./
</pre>

till I/ make PLAIN/ the MEAning/
of ALL/ my THOU/sand YEARS —/
till i FILL/ their HEARTS/ with KNOWledge,/
while i FILL/ their EYES/ with TEARS./   20
(Rudyard Kipling, "The Recall," 1909)

In addition to ten unrhymed feminine endings, used as a kind of
nonrhyming pattern for lines one and three of each stanza,
roughly one-sixth of this poem's sixty metrical feet are trisyllabic.
It is Chaucerian Compromise verse but, on prosodic grounds
alone, clearly of the nineteenth century (no matter what its
precise chronological tag).

e.   i MUST/ go DOWN/ to the SEAS/ aGAIN,/ to the
        LONE/ly SEA/ and the SKY,/
      and ALL/ i ASK/ is a TALL/ SHIP and/ a STAR/ to
        STEER/ her BY,/
      and the WHEEL'S/ KICK and/ the WIND'S/
        SONG, and/ the WHITE/ SAIL'S/ SHAking,/
      and a GREY/ MIST on/ the SEA'S FACE,/ and a
        GREY/ DAWN/ BREAking./

      i MUST/ go DOWN/ to the SEAS/ aGAIN,/ for the
        CALL/ of the RUN/ning TIDE   5
      is a WILD/ CALL and/ a CLEAR/ CALL that/
        MAY not/ BE/ deNIED;/
      and ALL/ i ASK/ is a WIN/dy DAY/ with the WHITE/
        CLOUDS/ FLYing,/
      and the FLUNG/ SPRAY and/ the BLOWN/
        SPUME, and/ the SEA/-GULLS/ CRYing./

      i MUST/ go DOWN/ to the SEAS/ aGAIN/ to the
        VA/grant GYP/sy LIFE,/
      to the GULL's/ WAY, and/ the WHALE'S/
        WAY where/ the WIND'S/ like a WHET/ted KNIFE;/ 10

and ALL/ i ASK/ is a MER/ry YARN/ from a
LAUGH/ing FEL/low-ROver,/
and a QUI/et SLEEP,/ and a SWEET/ DREAM when/
the LONG/ TRICK'S/ Over./
                          (John Masefield, "Sea-Fever," 1902)

Standard metrical marking, as here, in fact obscures the partially stress-determined prosody. In the poem's first stanza, e.g., Masefield's spondees—technically impossible in Chaucerian Compromise verse—are in fact seven in number ("TALL SHIP" in line two; "WHEEL'S KICK," "WIND'S SONG," and "WHITE SAIL'S," in line three; and "GREY MIST," "SEA'S FACE," and "GREY DAWN" in line four). Indeed, two of the seven are triple spondees — "WHITE SAIL'S SHAKing" and "GREY DAWN BREAKing," in lines three and four. Nor is it surprising, in poetry which thus leans backward toward the *Ur-Metrik* of the English language, that alliteration should come prominently to the fore. (There are six [w] words in line ten.)

f.   ISLED in/ the MID/night AIR,/
        MUSKED with/ the DARK'S/ faint BLOOM,/
        OUT in/to GLOOM/ing and SE/cret HAUNTS/
            the FLAME/ cries, "COME!"/

        LOVEly/ in DYE/ and FAN/   5
        aTREM/ble in SHIM/mering GRACE,/
        a MOTH/ from her WIN/ter SWOON/
            upLIFTS/ her FACE./

        STARES from/ her GLA/morous EYES;/
        WAFTS her/ on PLUMES/ like MIST;/   10
        in EC/stasy SWIRLS/ and SWAYS/
            to HER/ strange TRYST./
                    (Walter de la Mare, "The Moth," 1921)

In nine full-length lines (eight trimeter, one tetrameter), comprising a total of twenty-eight metrical feet, this apparently thoroughly conventional, regular-seeming poem has six trisyllabic feet.

g.   now LAMP/-lit GAR/dens IN/ the BLUE/ dusk SHINE/
        through DOG/-wood RED/ and WHITE,/
     and ROUND/ the GREY/ quadRANG/les, LINE/ by
        LINE,/
     the WIN/dows FILL/ with LIGHT,/
     where PRINCE/ton CALLS/ to MAG/dalen*, TO/wer to
        TOwer,/   5
     twin LANT/horns OF/ the LAW,/
     and THOSE/ cream-WHITE/ magNOL/ia BOUGHS/
        emBOwer/
     the HALLS/ of OLD/ nasSAU./ . . .

                     (Alfred Noyes, "Princeton," 1917: excerpt)

---

*British pronounciation = "MAUDlin"

The tepidities of the metrical frame seem to dictate the linguistic forcing of "quadRANgles" and "nasSAU," neither of which are possible as pronunciations. Which is of course once again the point: the poet is not working with pronunciation at all, but only with prosodic conventions grown stale and tired. This is not poetry meant to be heard as written; arguably, it is not meant to be heard at all, but only, like serious British drama of the nineteenth century, to be read. It is, in a word, as much "closet poetry" as the plays of Byron and Browning, of Wordsworth and Tennyson, are "closet drama."

h.   the RAIN/ and WIND,/ the RAIN/ and WIND,/ raved
        END/lessLY./
     on ME/ the SUM/mer STORM,/ and FE/ver and
        ME/lanCHOLy/
     wrought MA/gic, SO/ that IF/ i FEARED/ the
        SO/liTUDE/
     far MORE/ i FEARED/ all COM/paNY:/ too
        SHARP,/ too RUDE,/
     had BEEN/ the WI/sest OR/ the DEAR/est HU/man
        VOICE./   5
     what I/ deSIRED/ i KNEW/ not, BUT/ whatE'ER/
        my CHOICE/
     VAIN it/ must BE,/ i KNEW./ yet NAUGHT/ did MY/
        deSPAIR/
     *but sweeten the strange sweetness, while through the
        wild air*

155

ALL/ day LONG/ i HEARD/ a DIS/tant CUC/koo
    CALling/
and, SOFT/ as DUL/ciMERS,/ SOUNDS of/ near
    WA/ter FALling,/   10
and, SOF/ter, AND/ reMOTE/ as IF/ in HIS/toRY,/
RUmors/ of WHAT/ had TOUCHED/ my
    FRIENDS,/ my FOES,/ or ME./
            (Edward Thomas, "Melancholy," 1917)

It is worth speculating on the effect "whate'er" might have
produced on Edward Thomas himself, had anyone living actually
spoken it in his presence. The syntax too is moribund: to begin
line two with the awkward, half incomprehensible "on me" is
clearly Thomas' solution to problems of rhyme and meter, rather
than anything intended to resemble (or even approximate) normal
English usage. But when the poet and the language of his poem
are so separated from the language of their time that one feels
more in the presence of a creakingly reconstructed museum piece
than any sort of living voice, the conventions fueling poet and
poem alike are in serious trouble.

The only "hexameter" I can find in line eight is: "but SWEE/
ten the STRANGE/ SWEET/ness, while THROUGH/ the WILD/
AIR." The difficulty, plainly, is that while this scansion does
indeed have six metrical feet, it is not hexameter.

i. BREATHless,/ we FLUNG/ us ON/ the WIN/dy HILL,/
        LAUGHED in/ the SUN,/ and KISSED/ the
        LOVE/ly GRASS./
    you SAID,/ "through GLO/ry and EC/staSY/ we PASS;/
wind, SUN,/ and EARTH/ reMAIN,/ the BIRDS/ sing STILL,/
when WE/ are OLD,/ are OLD . . ."/ "and WHEN/ we DIE 5
    all's O/ver THAT/ is OURS;/ and LIFE/ burns ON/
through O/ther LO/vers, O/ther LIPS,"/ said I,/
"HEART of/ my HEART,/ our HEA/ven is NOW,/ is WON!"/

    "WE are/ earth's BEST,/ that LEARNT/ her
    LES/son HERE./
    LIFE is/ our CRY./ we have KEPT/ the
    FAITH!"/ we SAID./   10
    "WE shall/ go DOWN/ with UN/reLUCT/ant TREAD/

rose-CROWNED/ INto/ the DARK/ness!'' . . .
    PROUD/ we WERE,/
and LAUGHED,/ that HAD/ such BRAVE/ true
    THINGS/ to SAY./
—and THEN/ you SUD/denly CRIED,/ and
    TURNED/ aWAY./
               (Rupert Brooke, ''The Hill,'' 1908–1911)

The superficially placid metrics are in fact hard-won. ''We flung us,'' in the very first line, is as forced, as patently ''poetic,'' as most of the rest of Edwardian (and Brooke's own) verse. Substituting meaningless letters for words emphasizes the syntactical absurdity, and the over-inflated rhetoric, of line three: ''Through A and B we pass.'' Not only is the inversion at the end of line four awkward (normal usage requires ''the birds still sing'') but it suggests adjective/adverb confusion and a vexingly possible alternative meaning: the birds sing *quietly* (a legitimate sense for ''still'' as an adjective—and the positioning of adjectives, in English, tends to put them before rather than after the verb, except for the copula). ''All's over that is ours,'' in line six, is once again a never-never construct, linguistically quite impossible. And so on. Virtually the only linguistically possible line in the poem, indeed, is the superb final line: as George Edward Woodberry said, in introducing Brooke's *Collected Poems*, ''he knew how to end.'' (*The Collected Poems of Rupert Brooke*, New York, Dodd, Mead, 1926, p.9) Perhaps Brooke could have learned more, perhaps not; the latter seems more probable, since he was twenty-eight when he died, and poets grow old very young, when they grow old at all. The Edwardian context was not conducive to any manner of maturity except that of chronology.

j.   WE/ are THEY/ who DREAM/ no DREAMS,/
        SING/ers OF/ aRIS/ing DAY/
        WHO un/DAUNted,/
        WHERE/ the SWORD/ of REA/son GLEAMS,/
        FOL/low HARD,/ to HEW/ aWAY/   5
        the WOODS/ enCHANted./
        THROUGH/ each DARK/ and RUST/ling BYway/
        E/vil THINGS/ have FLED/ beFORE us:/
        WE pur/SUE them:/

WE/ have CARVED/ an O/pen HIGHway,/   10
WE/ have SUNG/ of TRUTH/ in CHOrus/
AS we/ SLEW them./

> (James Elroy Flecker, "Donde
> Estan?," 1909: excerpt)

Flecker's editor, J.C. Squire, wrote in the introduction to the *Collected Poems* (1928), that Flecker "thought that English verse was in danger of decomposition. He merely desired to emphasize the dangers both of prosing and of personal paroxysms; and, above all, to insist upon careful craftsmanship." (p.xxiv) Those opinions nicely summarize, and account for the insignificance of, the British Edwardian poets, as they also help to explain the banality of this poem. The poundingly awkward metrical sequence—tetrameter, tetrameter, dimeter, repeated four times—is insistently coupled with heaped-up inversions ("the woods enchanted" of line six is perhaps the most offensively silly). No artificiality, no bland generality, seems to have been avoided: this is truly a poet determined to say nothing and to say it with heroic blandness.

20 / Frost, Pound, Eliot, Williams

a. SOMEthing/ there IS/ that DOES/n't LOVE/ a WALL,/
    that SENDS/ the FRO/zen-GROUND/-swell UN/der IT
    and SPILLS/ the UP/per BOUL/ders IN/ the SUN,/
    and MAKES/ GAPS e/ven TWO/ can PASS/ aBREAST./
    the WORK/ of HUN/ters IS/ anO/ther THING:/   5
    I have/ come AF/ter THEM/ and MADE/ rePAIR
    where THEY/ have LEFT/ not ONE/ stone ON/ a
        STONE,/
    but THEY/ would HAVE/ the RAB/bit OUT/ of HIding,/
    to PLEASE/ the YEL/ping DOGS./ the GAPS/ i MEAN,/
    NO one/ has SEEN/ them MADE/ or HEARD/
        them MADE,/   10
    BUT at/ spring MEN/ding-TIME/ we FIND/ them
        THERE./
    i LET/ my NEIGH/bor KNOW/ beYOND/ the HILL;/
    and ON/ a DAY/ we MEET/ to WALK/ the LINE
    and SET/ the WALL/ beTWEEN/ us ONCE/ aGAIN./
    we KEEP/ the WALL/ beTWEEN/us AS/ we GO./ . . .   15
            (Robert Frost, "Mending Wall," 1914: excerpt)

If anyone could have saved traditional poetry largely untouched,
both in prosodic and in larger matters outside the scope of this
book, it would have been Frost. I think, on balance, Frost is most
sensibly regarded as the end, the consummation, and the tran-
scendent height of the conservative, even "academic" line of
American poetry that begins with William Cullen Bryant and

runs, over the better part of a century, through Longfellow, Lowell, Whittier, and their epigones, down to Edwin Arlington Robinson. But Frost has not turned out to be the "end," in the usual sense of the word: despite the apparently conclusive triumph of *vers libre*, poetry "in measures"—i.e., nontraditional but still Chaucerian-Compromise in essence—has not only continued to be written, but has of late made its presence fairly strongly felt. Frost epigones like Robert Francis have turned out not to Frost epigones at all, but major poets in their own right. And arguments have been made, notably by Frederick Turner (see especially "Performed Being: Word Art as a Human Inheritance," and "The Neural Lyre: Poetic Meter, The Brain, and Time,' in his *Natural Classicism*, N.Y., Paragon, 1985) which suggest compelling reasons why the Chaucerian Compromise must and will survive.

The deft handling of metrical irregularity, in lines like the fourth in this excerpt, and especially in line eleven, exhibit Frost's muscular lyricism at its very best. No one in England until Seamus Heanesy (see below, p.182), and perhaps not even Heaney, can handle Chaucerian Compromise prosody with this sort of power and suppleness.

b. What I am most interested in emphasizing . . . is the sentence of sound, because to me a sentence is not interesting merely in conveying a meaning in words. It must do something more; it must convey a meaning by sound. . . . Meter has to do with beat, and sound-posture has a definite relation as an alternate tone between the beats. The two are one in creation but separate in analysis. . . . It does not seem possible to me that a man can read on the printed page what he has never heard. Nobody today knows how to read Homer and Virgil perfectly, because the people who spoke Homer's Greek and Virgil's Latin are as dead as the sound of their language. . . . Poetry [today] has seized on this sound of speech and carried it to artificial and meaningless lengths. We have it exemplified in Sidney Lanier's musical notations of verse, where all the tones of the human voice in natural speech are entirely eliminated, leaving the sound of sense without root in experience.

(Frost, " . . . getting the sound of sense," 1915, in *Robert Frost: Poetry and Prose*, ed. Edward Connery Lathem and Lawrance Thompson, N.Y., Holt, Rinehart and Winston, 1972, pp.261–63)

c.   beFORE/ man CAME/ to BLOW/ it RIGHT/
        the WIND/ once BLEW/ itSELF/ unTAUGHT,/
     and DID/ its LOU/dest DAY/ and NIGHT/
        in A/ny ROUGH/ place WHERE/ it CAUGHT./

     man CAME/ to TELL/ it WHAT/ was WRONG:/   5
     it HAD/n't FOUND/ the PLACE/ to BLOW;/
     it BLEW/ too HARD/—the AIM/ was SONG./
        and LIST/en HOW/ it OUGHT/ to GO!/

     he TOOK/ a LIT/tle IN/ his MOUTH,/
        and HELD/ it LONG/ eNOUGH/ for NORTH/   10
     to BE/ conVER/ted IN/to SOUTH,
        and THEN/ by MEA/sure BLEW/ it FORTH./

     by MEA/sure. IT/ was WORD/ and NOTE,/
        the WIND/ the WIND/ had MEANT/ to BE —/
     a LIT/tle THROUGH/ the LIPS/ and THROAT./   15
        the AIM/ was SONG/—the WIND/ could SEE./
            (Frost, "The Aim was Song," 1923)

Consider simply the sinewy tension created as between natural
and prosodic stresses, in lines four and five of this deceptively
simple poem, or the thunderously deft caesura at the start of line
thirteen. There is literally no counterpart to such prosodic mastery, on the other side of the Atlantic, in any of Frost's contemporaries.

d.   whose WOODS/ these ARE/ i THINK/ i KNOW,/
     his HOUSE/ is IN/ the VIL/lage, THOUGH;/
     he WILL/ not SEE/ me STOP/ping HERE/
     to WATCH/ his WOODS/ fill UP/ with SNOW./

     my LIT/tle HORSE/ must THINK/ it QUEER/   5
     to STOP/ withOUT/ a FARM/house NEAR/
     beTWEEN/ the WOODS/ and FRO/zen LAKE/
     the DAR/kest EVE/ning OF/ the YEAR./

     he GIVES/ his HAR/ness BELLS/ a SHAKE/
     to ASK/ if THERE/ is SOME/ misTAKE./   10

the ON/ly O/ther SOUND'S/ the SWEEP/
of EA/sy WIND/ and DOW/ny FLAKE./

the WOODS/ are LOVE/ly, DARK,/ and DEEP,/
but I/ have PRO/miSES/ to KEEP,/
and MILES/ to GO/ beFORE/ i SLEEP,/   15
and MILES/ to GO/ beFORE/ i SLEEP./
(Frost, "Stopping by Woods on
a Snowy Evening," 1923)

e. "LAPpo/ i LEAVE/ beHIND/ and DAN/te TOO,/
lo, I/ would SAIL/ the SEAS/ with THEE/ aLONE!/
TALK me/ no LOVE/ talk, no BOUGHT/-cheap FID/dlRY,/
MINE is/ the SHIP/ and THINE/ the MER/chanDISE,/
all the blind earth knows not th'emprise   5
whereTO/ thou CALL/edst AND/ whereTO/ i CALL./

lo, I/ have SEEN/ thee BOUND/ aBOUT/ with DREAMS,/
lo, I/ have KNOWN/ thy HEART/ and ITS/ deSIRE;/
life, ALL/ of IT,/ my SEA,/ and ALL/ men's STREAMS/
are FUSED/ in IT/ as FLAMES/ of an AL/tar FIRE!/   10

lo, THOU/ hast VOY/aged NOT!/ the SHIP/ is MINE."
(Ezra Pound, "Guido Invites You Thus," 1909)

Pound took an unusually long time to mature, both prosodically and in other ways. But even in this early poem one can see, and not simply in the line I have marked as too prosodically uncertain for formal scansion, how Pound's ear was responding to the pull of cadences unfamiliar to nineteenth-century men generally. "Make it new," his great critical slogan, was formulated long before his poetry itself was able to even approximate the task. But the impulse was present from the start. (For a brief but distinctly conclusive comparison to the work of lesser Americans writing at this same time, see my *Ezra Pound: The Prime Minister of Poetry*, Hamden, Conn., Archon, 1984, pp.15–17.)

f.   "time's BIT/ter FLOOD!"/ oh, THAT'S/ all VE/ry
WELL,/
but WHERE'S/ the OLD/ friend HAS/n't FAL/len
OFF,/

or SLACKED/ his HAND/-grip WHEN/ you
   FIRST/ gripped FAME?/
i KNOW/ your CIR/cle AND/ can FAIR/ly TELL/
what YOU/ have KEPT/ and WHAT/ you've LEFT/
   beHIND:/   5
i KNOW/ my CIR/cle AND/ know VE/ry WEll/
how MA/ny FA/ces I'D/ have OUT/ of MIND./
          (Pound, "In Exitum Cuisdam: On a certain one's
                        departure," 1912)

Still essentially conventional in prosody, this somewhat more
mature poem shows that Pound, like Frost, knew a great deal
about the clash and clang of natural versus prosodic stress.

g. I suspect that Mr Housman suffers from a deficient curiosity.
Such as he has seems hardly to have led him to consider any
verse save that having good heavy swat on every alternate sylla-
ble, or least formed predominantly on the system of *ti TUM ti
TUM ti TUM*, sometimes up to ten syllables.
   (Pound, "Mr Housman at Little Bethel," 1914: excerpt)

h.   like a SKEIN of LOOSE SILK BLOWN aGAINST
         a WALL
      she WALKS by the RAILing of a PATH in
         KENsington GARdens,
      and SHE is DYing PIECEmeal
         of a SORT of eMOtional aNEMia.

      and ROUND aBOUT there is a RABble   5
      of the FILthy, STURdy, unKILLable INfants
         of the VEry POOR.
      THEY shall inHErit the EARTH.

      in HER is the END of BREEDing.
      her BOREdom is exQUIsite and exCESsive.
      she would LIKE SOME one to SPEAK to her,   10
      and is ALmost aFRAID that I
         will comMIT that INdisCREtion.
                   (Pound, "The Garden," 1916)

Four years later, plainly, Pound has discarded formal prosodic feet in favor of a strong, lyrical stress-based line. How much this new prosody owes to the old can be debated; it is more than possible to argue that this is not in fact *vers libre* (an argument that T.S. Eliot among others indeed made at the time). But it is not possible to dispute that Pound has indeed here "made it new."

i.   the APpaRItion of these FAces in the CROWD;
       PEtals on a WET, BLACK BOUGH.
                      (Pound, "In a Station of the Metro," 1916)

The two signal facts about this little poem, prosodically, are (1) that it has four stresses in each of its lines but (2) varies from twelve syllables in the first to seven syllables in the second of those lines. In a very real sense, these two facts encapsulate the thirteen- or fourteen-hundred year history of prosody in our language.

j. It is too late to prevent vers libre. But, conceivably, one might improve it, and one might stop at least a little of the idiotic and narrow discussion based on an ignorance of music. Bigoted attack, born of this ignorance of the tradition of music, was what we had to live through.
       (Pound, "Vers Libre and Arnold Dolmetsch," 1918: excerpt)

k. In making a line of verse (and thence building the lines into passages) you have certain primal elements:
       That is to say, you have the various "articulate sounds" of the language, of its alphabet, that is, and the various groups of letters in syllables.
       These syllables have differing weights and durations
       A. original weights and durations
       B. weights and durations that seem naturally imposed on them by the other syllable groups around them.

Those are the medium wherewith the poet cuts his design in TIME. . . . The writer of bad verse is a bore because he does not perceive time and time relations, and cannot therefore delimit them in an interesting manner, by means of longer and shorter,

164

heavier and lighter syllables, and the varying qualities of sound inseparable from the words of his speech. . . . [Prosodic] nomenclatures were probably invented by people who had never LISTENED to verse, and who probably wouldn't have been able to distinguish Dante's movement from Milton's had they heard it read aloud.

Pound, *ABC of Reading*, London, Faber, 1951, pp.198–99, 204

l.   m'aMOUR, m'aMOUR
            WHAT do i LOVE and
                    WHERE ARE YOU?
        that i LOST my CENter
            FIGHTing the WORLD.
        the DREAMS CLASH
                and are SHATtered —
        and that i TRIED to MAKE a PAraDIso

        teREStre.

                            (Pound, Notes for Cantos
                            CXVII et seq.,'' before 1969)

Anyone who doubts that, to the very end, Pound was capable of lyrical flashes of brilliant intensity should read and re-read, and then pause to analyze the verse movement, of these incredibly poignant lines. Let me quote, briefly, from my *Ezra Pound*:

> "Where are you living now?" a reporter asked him, toward the end of his life. "In hell," was Pound's reply. The journalist persisted. "Which hell?" And the poet, pressing his hands to his heart, mouthed the words, "Here, here." (p.14)

m. LET us/ GO then,/ YOU/ and I,/
    WHEN/ the EVE/ning IS/ spread OUT/ aGAINST/ the
        SKY/
    LIKE/ a PA/tient E/theRISED/ upON/ a TAble;/
    LET us/ GO,/ through CER/tain HALF/-deSER/ted
        STREETS,/
    the MUT/terING/ reTREATS/   5
    of REST/less NIGHTS/ in ONE/-night CHEAP/ hoTELS/
    and SAW/dust RE/stauRANTS/ with OY/ster-SHELLS:/

STREETS/ that FOL/low LIKE/ a TE/dious*
  AR/guMENT/
of inSI/diOUS/ inTENT/
to LEAD/ you TO/ an O/verWHELM/ing QUEStion . . .   10
oh, DO/ not ASK,/ "what IS it?"/
LET us/ GO/ and MAKE/ our VIsit./

In/ the ROOM/ the WO/men COME/ and GO/
TALKing/ of MI/chaelAN/geLO./ . . .

(T.S. Eliot, "The Love Song of
J. Alfred Prufrock," 1917: excerpt)

---

*bisyllabic?

The 1948 comment by Sister M. Martin Barry, O.P., that "Considered from the standpoint of prosodic structure, [Eliot's] poems are not startling in their innovations," remains on the whole perfectly valid. (Barry, *An Analysis of the Prosodic Structure of Selected Poems of T.S. Eliot*, Washington, D.C., Catholic University of America Press, 1969, p.105) Iambic trimeter, tetrameter, pentameter, and hexameter are freely handled, here, with a good many trochaic feet interspersed, and line lengths are freely alternated, according to essentially ad hoc patterns. Rhyme too is sometimes perfect, sometimes omitted: only in the final twelve lines of this one hundred and thirty-one-line poem does the rhyming suddenly become insistent.

n.   HERE i AM, an OLD MAN in a DRY MONTH,
     being READ to by a BOY, WAITing for RAIN.
     i was NEIther at the HOT GATES
     nor FOUGHT in the WARM RAIN
     nor KNEE DEEP in the SALT MARSH, HEAving a
       CUTlass,   5
     BITten by FLIES, FOUGHT. . . .

(Eliot, "Gerontion," 1920: excerpt)

But only a very few years down the road, Eliot, like Pound, has clearly felt, and responded to, the pounding, distinctly untraditional cadences of our century. It is the farthest thing from accidental that, the next year, the titanic, savage rhythms of

Stravinsky's *Le Sacre du Printemps* powerfully affected Eliot, and heavily influenced the rhythms of *The Waste Land*. (See my *T.S. Eliot*, N.Y., Continuum/Ungar, 1982, 1991, p.73).

o. Vers libre [free verse] does not exist. . . . [it] has not even the excuse of a polemic; it is a battle-cry of freedom, and there is no freedom in art. And as the so-called *vers libre* which is good is anything but "free," it can better be defended under some other label. . . . What sort of a line that would be which would not scan at all I cannot say. . . . Any line can be divided into feet and accents. . . . [But] scansion tells us very little. . . . The most interesting verse which has yet been written in our language has been done either by taking a very simple form, like the iambic pentameter, and constantly withdrawing from it, or taking no form at all, and constantly approximating to a very simple one. It is this contrast between fixity and flux, this unperceived evasion of monotony, which is the very life of verse. . . . Freedom is only truly freedom when it appears against the background of an artificial limitation. . . . There is no escape from metre; there is only mastery.

(Eliot, "Reflections on Vers Libre," 1917, in Eliot, *To Criticize the Critic*, London, Faber, 1965, pp.183–88)

p. MAdame/ soSOS/tris, FA/mous CLAIR/voyANTE,/
    HAD a/ bad COLD,/ NEver/theLESS/
    is KNOWN/ to BE/ the WI/sest WO/man in EUrope,/
    with a WIC/ked PACK/ of CARDS./ HERE/ said SHE,/
    is YOUR/ card, the DROWNED/ phoeNI/cian
        SAIlor,/   5
    (THOSE/ are PEARLS/ that WERE/ his EYES./
        LOOK!)/
    HERE/ is BEL/laDON/na, the LA/dy of the ROCKS,/
    the LA/dy of SI/tuAtions./
    HERE is/ the MAN/ with three STAVES,/ and
        HERE/ the WHEEL,/
    and HERE/ is the ONE/-eyed MER/chant, and THIS
        CARD,/   10
    which is BLANK,/ is SOME/thing he CAR/ries on his
        BACK,/
    which I/ am forBID/den to SEE./ i DO/ not FIND/

167

the HANGED/ MAN./ fear DEATH/ by WAter./
i see CROWDS/ of PEO/ple, WALK/ing ROUND/ in a
RING./ . . .
(Eliot, "The Waste Land," 1922: excerpt)

This can obviously be scanned. But equally obviously, it is not the Chaucerian Compromise verse of Spenser, or even that of Milton. Eliot feels obligated only to his poem, not to the traditions behind it. He departs from "rules" with a freedom so complete that it is neither arbitrary nor disputable: it is utterly authoritative, with itself as its only necessary underpinning.

q. i DO/ not know MUCH/ about GODS;/ but i THINK/ that
the RIver/
is a STRONG/ brown GOD —/ SULlen,/ unTAMED/
and inTRACtable,/
PAtient/ to SOME/ deGREE,/ at FIRST/
REcog/nized AS/ a fronTIER;/
USEful,/ unTRUST/worthy, AS/ a conVEY/or of
COMmerce;
then ON/ly a PROB/lem conFRONT/ing the BUIL/der
of BRIDges./ . . .   5
(Eliot, "The Dry Salvages," 1941: excerpt)

Whatever its rhetorical weaknesses, this late poem exhibits much the same prosodic authority, handling the intractable with such ease that it becomes both flexible and, still more important, musically *interesting*. Of what British poet during this same period can as much be said? (Yeats is of course not British but Irish.)

r.   at TEN A.M. the YOUNG HOUSEwife
MOVES aBOUT in NEgligee beHIND
the WOOden WALLS of her HUSband's HOUSE.
i PASS SOliTAry in my CAR.

THEN aGAIN she COMES to the CURB   5
to CALL the ICE-man, FISH-man, and STANDS
SHY, unCORseted, TUCking IN

stray ENDS of HAIR, and I comPARE her
to a FALlen LEAF.

the NOISEless WHEELS of my CAR   10
RUSH with a CRACKling SOUND Over
DRIED LEAVES as i BOW and PASS SMIling.
(William Carlos Williams, "The Young Housewife,"
1917)

Williams' prosody is deeply unlike that of either Pound or Eliot.
From the beginning, Williams knows the music he is after, the
sounds and above all the pace of a basically urban, basically
mechanized America. It is not too much to say, I think, that the
rhythm of "The Young Housewife" is in good part the rhythm of
the automobile being driven by the poem's persona—and neither
Tennyson nor Browning could possibly have experieinced anything like it, much less lived it, as Williams did, every day of his
mature life.

A basic but prosodically unclassifiable tetrameter dominates;
only the final lines of two strophes (a word I use, in this context,
to mean a verse division which is non-replicative and therefore
cannot properly be called a "stanza") break the overall pattern,
in line nine with a dimeter, in line twelve, the poem's last line,
with a pentameter. Clearly, however, it is less confusing to avoid
such tradition-laden terms, here, and simply call this a poem with
four stresses per line as its basic pattern, one of its twelve lines
having two stresses, and one having five.

s.   OLD AGE is
                a FLIGHT of SMALL
                CHEEping BIRDS
                SKIMming
                BARE TREES   5
                aBOVE a SNOW GLAZE.
                GAINing and FAILing
                THEY are BUFfeted
                by a DARK WIND—
                but WHAT?   10
                on HARSH WEEDstalks
                the FLOCK has RESted,

169

the SNOW
is COvered with BROken
SEEDhusks   15
and the WIND TEMpered
by a SHRILL
PIping of PLENty.
                    (Williams, "To Waken
                    An Old Lady"), 1921)

Although this does not pulse to the same beat as the poems of
Pound and Eliot, it pulses quite as much as it flows. Again, ours
is the century of the staccato; it is not accidental that as many
people accept the voice of Pound, or the voice of Eliot, or the
voice of Williams as *the* archetypical poetic voice of our time.
Who could make, or exult in, a similar statement about, say,
James Elroy Flecker?

t. Verse—we'd better not speak of poetry lest we become confused — verse has always been associated in men's minds with
"measure," i.e., with mathematics. In scanning any piece of
verse, you "count" the syllables. Let's not speak either of
rhythm, an aimless sort of thing without precise meaning of any
sort. But measure implies something that can be measured. Today
verse has lost all measure.
    Our lives also have lost all that in the past we had to measure
them by, except outmoded standards that are meaningless to us.
In the same way our verses, of which our poems are made, are
left without any metrical construction of which you can speak,
any recognizable, any new measure by which they can be pulled
together. We get sonnets, etc., but no one alive today, or half
alive, seems to see anything incongruous in that. They cannot
see that poems cannot any longer be made following a Euclidian
measure, "beautiful" as this may make them. The very grounds
for our beliefs have altered. We do not live that way any more;
nothing in our lives, at bottom, is ordered according to that
measure; our social concepts, our schools, our very religious
ideas, certainly our understanding of mathematics are greatly
altered. Were we called upon to go back to what we believed in
the past we should be lost. Only the construction of our poems—
and at best the construction of a poem must engage the tips of
our intellectual awareness—is left shamefully to the past.

. . . The thing is that "free verse" since Whitman's time has led us astray. . . . Whitman was right in breaking our bounds but, having no valid restraints to hold him, went wild. He didn't know any better. At the last he resorted to a loose sort of language with no discipline about it of any sort and we have copied its worst features, just that.

. . . No verse can be free, it must be governed by some measure, but not by the old measure. . . . We have to return to some measure but a measure consonant with our time and not a mode so rotten that it stinks.

[And] we have no measure by which to guide ourselves except a purely intuitive one which we feel but do not name.
(Williams, "On Measure," 1953: excerpt)

u.   so MUCH dePENDS
                            upON

                            a RED WHEEL
                            BARrow

                            GLAZED with RAIN   5
                            WAter

                            beSIDE the WHITE
                            CHICkens.
                                (Williams, "The Red
                                Wheelbarrow," 1923)

Like the smear of primary pigment across a stark white canvas, Williams *splays* his poem quite as much as he *writes* it. This is of course not the place to make the demonstration, but a thorough analysis of the express and implied esthetic(s) of this poem, and virtually anything written by Geoffrey Chaucer, should make abundantly clear why their prosodies are at opposite linguistic poles. Indeed, since differences in degree become, at a certain point, differences in kind, a valid argument can be made, I think, that what Williams in particular is up to is not poetry at all, in the sense with which that word reverberated for Chaucer. I hope it is not necessary to emphasize that this is not a pejorative statement as to either poet, but simply a descriptive one.

v. in BREUghel's GREAT PICture, the KERMESS,
    the DANcers go ROUND, they go ROUND and
    aROUND, the SQUEAL and the BLARE and the
    TWEEdle of BAGpipes, a BUgle and FIDdles
    TIPping their BELlies (ROUND as the THICK-   5
    SIded GLASses whose WASH they imPOUND)
    their HIPS and their BELlies off BAlance
    to TURN them. KICking and ROLling aBOUT
    the FAIR GROUNDS, SWINGing their BUTTS, those
    SHANKS must be SOUND to BEAR up UNder such   10
    ROLlicking MEAsures, PRANCE as they DANCE
    in BREUghel's GREAT PICture, the KERMESS.
                        (Williams, "The Dance," 1944)

Again, it is readily possible to argue, as many commentators
indeed have, that if Pound is "new," Williams' poetry is new-
new. What has come to be called the "breath-line" of "The
dance" is not so much onomatopoeia—that is, a mirroring of the
physical pounding of the dance proper—so much as it is a
prosodic rendering of the poet's "breathless" response to that
physical pounding. This may seem an over-subtle distinction, but
in terms of what twentieth-century science has been teaching us
about the human impact on both subatomic and on cosmological
physics, as well as the other scientific realms, it is a distinction
of powerful effect and with deep consequences.

In prosodic terms, the section which follows, virtually without
comment, illustrates some of the other applications of twentieth-
century American poetic theory to a variety of verse possibilities.
The field is too large to be covered in this book. I include section
21, accordingly, with some hesitation and only to hint at what I
cannot here hope to properly deal with.

21 / Ten 20th-Century American Poets

a. it's JOLly
    ODD what POPS into
    your JOLly TETE when the
    JOLly SHELLS beGIN DROPping JOLly FAST you
    HEAR the RRMP and
    then NEARerandNEARerand N E A R e r
    and beFORE
    you can

    !

    & we're

    N O T
    (OH—
    —i SAY

    that's JOLly ODD
    old THING, JOLly
    ODD, JOLly
    JOLly ODD ISn't
    it JOLly ODD.

    (e e cummings, *IS 5*, poem Two: IV, 1926)

b.   the KNOWledge NOT of SORrow, YOU were
        SAYing, BUT of BOREdom

                                173

IS—aSIDE from REAding SPEAking
        SMOking —
of WHAT, maude BLESsingBOURNE it WAS,
        WISHED to KNOW WHEN, HAving RIsen,
"apPROACHED the WINdow as IF to SEE
        WHAT REALly was GOing ON";
and SAW RAIN FALling, in the DIStance
        more SLOWly,
the ROAD CLEAR from HER PAST the WINdow
        GLASS ——
of the WORLD, WEAther-SWEPT, with WHICH
        one SHARES the CENtury.
                        (George Oppen, *Discrete Series*,
                                untitled poem, 1932–34)

c.   I, TOO, disLIKE it.
      REAding, howEver, with a PERfect conTEMPT for it,
      ONE disCOvers IN
      it, AFter ALL, a PLACE for the GENuine.
                        (Marianne Moore, "Poetry," 1935)

Miss Moore sometimes wrote, or thought she wrote, in a syllabic
prosody. That is of course an impossibility in English, as it is
equally impossible to know when she was and when she wasn't
attempting the impossible. This final version of her most famous
and much-revised poem on poetry does not appear to have a
syllabically-intended prosody. But I can't be sure. Who could?

d.   i SAW the BEST MINDS of MY geneRAtion
      desTROYED by MADness, STARving hySTErical
      NAked,
      DRAGging themSELVES through the NEgro
      STREETS at DAWN LOOking for an ANgry FIX,
      ANgelHEAded HIPsters BURning for the ANcient
      HEAvenly conNECtion to the STARry DYnamo in
      the maCHInery of NIGHT,

174

who POverty and TATters and HOLlow-EYED and
HIGH SAT UP SMOking in the SUperNAtural
DARKness of COLD-water FLATS FLOATing
aCROSS the TOPS of CIties CONtemPLATing
JAZZ,
who BARED their BRAINS to HEAven UNder the EL
and SAW moHAMmedan ANgels STAGgering on
TEnement ROOFS ilLUminated,   5
who PASSED through UniVERsities with RAdiant
COOL EYES halLUcinating ARkansas and BLAKE-
LIGHT TRAgedy aMONG the SCHOlars of WAR,
who were exPELLED from the aCAdemies for CRAzy
and PUBlishing obSCENE ODES on the WINdows
of the SKULL,
who COwered in unSHAven ROOMS in UNderWEAR,
BURning their MOney in WASTEbaskets and
LISTening to the TERror THROUGH the WALL,
who got BUSted in their PUbic BEARDS reTURning
THROUGH laREdo with a BELT of mariJUAna for
new YORK,
who ATE FIRE in PAINT hoTELS or DRANK
TURpentine in PAradise ALley, DEATH, or
PURgatoried their TORsos NIGHT after NIGHT   10
with DREAMS, with DRUGS, with WAking
NIGHTmares, ALcoHOL and COCK and ENDless
BALLS . . .
                    (Allen Ginsberg, "Howl," 1956: excerpt)

e.   the SO-called WILD HORses of the WAter
            STUMbled all Over the BOULders
            and FELL STEAMing and FOAMing Over
            the WORLD'S EDGE DOWN the ROARing
            WHITE WAY of the WAterFALL   5
            INto the BLACK POOL of the DEATH
            of MOtion at the BOTtom WHERE
            the COLD STONED WAter LAY
            DENSE as a DIAmond of PRESsure and
            the EYE of SIlence STARED unMOVED   10
            at the WORLD'S CAvalry FALling IN
            to BE the SEer NOT the HEARD aGAIN.
                        (Alan Dugan, "The So-Called Wild
                            Horses of the Water," 1961)

175

f. HENry, EDGED, deCIdedly, MADE up STOries
    LIGHTing the PAST of HENry, of his GLOrious
    PREsent, and his HOAries,
    ALL the BIGHT HEALS he TAMPED—euPHOria,
    MISter BONES, euPHOria. FATE CLOBber ALL.   5
    —HAND me BACK my CRAWL,

    conDIGN HEAven. TIGHten into a BALL
    eLONgate and VALVED HENry. TUCK him PEACE.
    RENder him SIGHTless,
    or RUin at HIGH RATE his CRAMpon FOcus,   10
    WIPE out his NEED. reDUCE him to the REST of US.
    —BUT, BONES, you IS that.

    —i CANnot reMEMber. i am GOing aWAY.
    there was SOMEthing in my DREAM aBOUT a CAT,
    which FOUGHT and SANG.   15
    SOMEthing aBOUT a LYRE, an ISLAND. unSTRUNG.
    LINKED to the LAND at low TIDE. CAbles FRAY.
    THANK you for EVErything.
              (John Berryman, *77 Dream Songs*, Poem 25, 1964)

g.   I have been STANDing ALL my LIFE in the
        diRECT PATH of a BATtery of SIGnals
        the MOST ACcurately transMITted MOST
        UNtransLAtable LANguage in the Universe
        I am a gaLACtic CLOUD so DEEP so INvo-   5
        LUTed that a LIGHT wave could TAKE FIFteen
        YEARS to TRAvel THROUGH me and HAS
        TAken I am an INstrument in the SHAPE
        of a WOman TRYing to TRANSlate pulSAtions
        INto Images for the reLIEF of the BOdy   10
        and the REconSTRUCtion of the MIND.
              (Adrienne Rich, ''Planetarium,'' 1968: excerpt)

h.   LIFE purSUED DOWN these CLIFFS.
        the Omened BIRDS
        inTRUsion; SKAted, at NIGHT
        CLEAR WAVES of WEAther
        FUR YOU I bring GENius   5

                          176

over HELL'S curiOsity
the liBRArian SHABbily books ON
you CANnot ilLUsion; the DUST.
ABstract VERmin the GARden WORN SMILES.
(John Ashbery, "Europe," section 19, 1962: excerpt)

i.   ENter this ROOM, if you WILL,
but SIlently.
it will SEEM EMPty,
but a WHITE FOX
and a BLACK FOX   5
are MAting
on the CRIMson RUG.
a NUMber of GOLD apPOINTments are FEAtured
in this ROOM
which you MUST not TOUCH,   10
and the FURniture is TOO VALuable to SIT on.
howEver,
we DO underSTAND your WISH
to SEE this PLACE,
to BREATHE the INcense,   15
and to apPREciate ITS traDItion.
IF you are INterested in the BLACK FOX
or the WHITE FOX
YOU may inSPECT them CLOSEly
and ASK ME Any QUEStions   20
you may HAVE. . . .
(Diane Wakoski, "Tour," 1962: excerpt)

j.   if i CAN'T HOPE then to HELL with it.
I don't WANT to LIVE like THIS?

like THIS, he SAID. WHERE WERE YOU?
SHE was aROUND in BACK of the BUReau

WHERE he PUSHED HER?
HELL NO, SHE just FELL.
(Robert Creeley, "Entre Nous," 1956–58)

177

22 / Five 20th-Century British Poets

a.   how CAN/ i, THAT/ girl STAN/ding THERE,/
     MY/ atTEN/tion FIX/
     on RO/man OR/ on RUSsian/
     OR/ on SPAN/ish PO/liTICS?
     yet HERE'S/ a TRA/velled MAN/ that KNOWS/   5
     WHAT/ he TALKS/ aBOUT,/
     and THERE'S/ a PO/liTIcian/
     THAT/ has READ/ and THOUGHT,/
     and MAY/be WHAT/ they SAY/ is TRUE/
     of WAR/ and WAR'S/ aLARMS,/   10
     but O/ that I/ were YOUNG/ aGAIN/
     and HELD her IN/ my ARMS!/
          (William Butler Yeats, "Politics," 1936–39)

Any instrument can be well tuned; so too can any language. But an essential secret of the tuning process is knowing what the particular instrument can and cannot be made to do. And in working with a language, the possibilities are both infinite and restricted: given its syntactical arrangements, its lexical possibilities, its phonology, and so on, every language is *within its boundaries* infinite. Yet just as the greatest mystics have always operated within a specific parochial tradition, so too the poet's exploitation of a language must remain within that language's boundaries.

And no one, surely, has ever better exploited the traditional possibilities of English better than Yeats.

b. NOW/ as I/ was YOUNG/ and EA/sy UN/der the AP/ple
            BOUGHS/
        aBOUT/ the LILT/ing HOUSE/ and HAP/py AS/ the
            GRASS/ was GREEN,/
        the NIGHT/ aBOVE/ the DIN/gle STARry,
                time LET/ me HAIL/ and CLIMB/
        GOL/den IN/ the HEY/days OF/ his EYES,/   5
        and HO/nored aMONG/ WAgons/ I was/ PRINCE of/
            the AP/ple TOWNS/
        and ONCE/ beLOW/ a TIME/ i LORD/ly HAD/
            the TREES/ and LEAVES/
                TRAIL/ with DAI/sies and BARley/
        DOWN/ the RI/vers OF/ the WIND/fall
            LIGHT./ . . .
                (Dylan Thomas, "Fern Hill," 1946: excerpt)

Unusually sequenced though it may be (most heptameter, or
seven-footed, verse breaks pretty readily into tetrameter and
trimeter segments, nor is most heptameter verse mixed with lines
of varying length), Thomas' verse is still prosodically founded in
the Chaucerian Compromise. But there are strongly alliterative
elements, harkening back to the *Ur-Metrik* of Old English. And
there are idiosyncratic syntactical arrangements, as also there
are unique rhetorical effects, which help make Thomas' version
of Chaucerian Compromise verse very much his own. Whatever
its range, this is clearly neither derivative nor tepid poetry.

c. aBOUT/ SUFfer/ing THEY/ were NE/ver WRONG,/
        the OLD/ MASters:/ how WELL/ they
            UN/derSTOOD/
        its HU/man poSI/tion; HOW/ it TAKES/ PLACE/
        while SOME/one ELSE/ is EAT/ing or OPE/ning a
            WIN/dow OR/ just
                WALK/ing DUL/ly aLONG;/
        HOW, when/ the A/ged are RE/verently, PAS/sionately
            WAITing/   5
        FOR the/ miRA/culous BIRTH,/ there AL/ways must
            BE/
        CHILdren/ who DID/ not SPEcially WANT/ it to
            HAP/pen, SKATing/

                        179

on a POND/ at the EDGE/ of the WOOD:/
they NE/ver forGOT/
that E/ven the DREAD/ful MAR/tyrDOM/ must RUN/ its
    COURSE/   10
Any/how IN/ a
    COR/ner, SOME/ unTI/dy SPOT/
where the DOGS/ go ON/ with their DOG/gy LIFE/ and
    the TOR/turer's HORSE/
SCRATches/ its IN/noCENT/ beHIND/ on a
    TREE./ . . .
            (W.H. Auden, "Musée des Beaux Arts," 1940: excerpt)

Prosody is no more than one technical aspect of Auden's early greatness as a poet. But surely the easy, flexible sequencing (anywhere from two to eight feet in a line, though the preponderance of the lines continue to be pentameter: we never know when to expect a variation) contributes to the understated drama he achieves. Again, this is Chaucerian Compromise verse, but the poet makes it clear that he takes prosodic requirements only as seriously as he happens to feel like—or not to feel like. There are no straitjackets in Auden's early verse.

d.   TALKing/ in BED/ OUGHT to/ be EAsiest,/
     LYing/ toGE/ther THERE/ goes BACK/ so FAR,/
     an EM/blem OF/ two PEO/ple BE/ing HOnest.

     yet MORE/ and MORE/ time PASS/es SI/lentLY.
     outSIDE,/ the WIND'S/ INcom/PLETE/ unREST/   5
     BUILDS and/ disPER/ses CLOUDS/ aBOUT/ the SKY./

     and DARK/ TOWNS/ heap UP/ ON the/ hoRIzon./
     NONE of/ this CARES/ for US./ NOthing/ shows WHY/
     at THIS/ unIQUE/ DIStance/ from I/soLAtion/

     it beCOMES/ STILL/ more DIF/ficult to FIND/   10
     WORDS/ at ONCE/ TRUE/ and KIND,/
     or NOT/ unTRUE/ and NOT/ unKIND./
             (Philip Larkin, "Talking in Bed," 1964)

Just like his fairly casual use of end-rhyme, Larkin's use of Chaucerian Compromise prosody is determinedly flippant-seeming. Not until the last two lines of this poem, indeed, is there a true metrical pattern, in the conventional sense, nor full rhyming, either. Those final lines, and the fact that the bulk of the poem *can* be conventionally scanned, suggest that the poem as a whole should be marked as containing metrical feet. But except for the two final lines I think it would make no particular difference were feet divisions to be omitted: for ten of its twelve lines, this is poetry that could about as properly be called vers libre as Chaucerian Compromise verse.

e. i SAT/ all MOR/ning IN/ the COL/lege SICK bay/
COUNting/ BELLS/ KNELLing/ CLASses/ to a
CLOSE./
at TWO/ o'CLOCK/ our NEIGH/bor DROVE/ me HOME./

IN the/ PORCH/ i MET/ my FA/ther CRYing —/
HE had/ ALways/ TAken/ FUnerals/ in his STRIDE —/   5
and BIG/ jim E/vans SAY/ing IT/ was a HARD/ BLOW./

the BA/by COOED/ and LAUGHED/ and ROCKED/ the
PRAM/
when I/ came IN,/ and I/ was emBARrassed
by OLD/ men STAND/ing UP/ to SHAKE/ my HAND/

and TELL/ me THEY/ were "SOR/ry FOR/ my
TROUble,"/   10
WHISpers/ inFORMED/ STRANgers/ I was/ the
ELDest,/
aWAY/ at SCHOOL,/ as my MO/ther HELD/ my HAND/

in HERS/ and COUGHED/ out AN/gry TEAR/less
SIGHS./
at TEN/ o'CLOCK/ the AM/buLANCE/ arRIVED/
WITH the/CORPSE,/ STANCHED and/ BANdaged/ by
the NURses./   15

181

next MOR/ning i WENT/ up IN/to the ROOM./
  SNOWdrops/
and CAN/dles SOOTHED/ the BED/side; I/ saw HIM/
for the FIRST/ TIME in/ six WEEKS./ PA/ler
  NOW,/

WEARing/ a POP/py BRUISE/ ON his/left TEMple,/
he LAY/ in the FOUR/ foot BOX/ as IN/ his COT./   20
no GAU/dy SCARS,/ the BUM/per KNOCKED/ him
  CLEAR./
a FOUR/ foot BOX,/ a FOOT/ for EVE/ry YEAR./
                    (Seamus Heaney, "Mid-Term Break," 1966)

In places, the scansion here marked is uncertain; it would be easy to trace out differing patterns, for it is not clear according to what mold the lines might have been cast. Like the last few poems, much of this could be either loose, relaxed Chaucerian Compromise verse or, about equally arguably, vers libre. I have chosen to treat it as conventional prosody because some of the lines are unmistakeably traditional, and also because there is a sense, throughout, that even if this is not standard Chaucerian Compromise verse—as clearly it is not—the poet remains always aware of the traditional standard, both when he complies with and when he departs from it.

Works Cited and Recommended

Editions of poetry and prosodic declarations by the poets are not here included.

Adams, Robert Martin, *Milton and the Modern Critics* (Ithaca, Cornell U. Press, 1955).

Barry, Sister M. Martin, *An Analysis of the Prosodic Structure of Selected Poems of T.S. Eliot* (Washington, D.C., Catholic U. of America Press, 1969).

Bowra, Maurice, "Foreword," in Bacchylides, *Complete Poems*, trans. Robert Fagles (New Haven, Yale U. Press, 1961).

Brogan, T.V.F., *English Versification, 1570–1980: A Reference Guide* . . . (Baltimore, Johns Hopkins U. Press, 1981).

Buxton, John, ed., *Poems of Michael Drayton* (Cambridge, Mass., Harvard U. Press, 1953).

Cable, Thomas, *The Meter and Melody of* Beowulf (Chicago, U. of Illinois Press, 1974).

Fraser, G.S., *Metre, Rhyme and Free Verse* (London, Methuen, 1970).

Fussell, Paul, *Poetic Meter and Poetic Form*, rev. ed. (N.Y., Random House, 1979).

Gross, Harvey, *Sound and Form in Modern Poetry* (Ann Arbor, U. of Michigan Press, 1964).

Gross, Harvey, ed., *The Structure of Verse: Modern Essays on Prosody* (N.Y., Fawcett, 1966).

Hall, Donald, ed., *Claims for Poetry* (Ann Arbor, U. of Michigan Press, 1982).

Hall, Robert A., Jr., *Introductory Linguistics* (Philadelphia, Chilton, 1964).

183

Halle, Morris, and Samuel Jay Keyser, *English Stress: Its Form, Its Growth, and Its Role in Verse* (N.Y., Harper, 1971).

Harding, D.W., "The Poetry of Wyatt," in *The Age of Chaucer*, ed. Boris Ford (Harmondsworth, Penguin, 1965).

Hartman, Charles O., *Free Verse: An Essay on Prosody* (Princeton U. Press, 1980).

Hollander, John, *Rhyme's Reason*, enlarged ed. (New Haven. Yale U. Press, 1989).

Isaacs, Neil D., *Structural Principles in Old English Poetry*, Knoxville, U. of Tennessee Press, 1968).

Jerome, Judson, *Poetry: Premeditated Art* (Boston, Houghton, Mifflin, 1968).

Jones, Emrys, ed., Henry Howard, Earl of Surrey, *Poems* (Oxford U. Press, 1964).

Kinsman, Philip, "Introduction," in John Skelton, *Poems*, ed. Philip Kinsman (Oxford U. Press, 19169).

Kostelanetz, Richard, *The Old Poetries and the New* (Ann Arbor, U. of Michigan Press, 1981).

Ladefoged, Peter, *A Course in Phonetics* (N.Y., Harcourt Brace Jovanovich, 1982).

Legouis, Emile, and Louis Cazamian, *A History of English Literature* (N.Y., Macmillan, 1929).

Muir, Kenneth, ed., *Collected Poems of Sir Thomas Wyatt* (London, Routledge and Kegan Paul, 1949).

Nash, Walter, *Our Experience of Language* (N.Y., St. Martin's, 1971).

Neilson, W.A. and K.G.T. Webster, *Chief British Poets of the Fourteenth and Fifteenth Centuries* (Boston, Houghton Mifflin, 1916).

Nist, John, *A Structural History of English* (N.Y., St. Martin's, 1966).

Norman, Charles, ed., *Poets on Poetry* (N.Y., Free Press, 1962).

Norton-Smith, John, ed., John Lydgate, *Poems* (Oxford U.Press, 1966).

Perkins, George, ed., *American Poetic Theory* (N.Y., Holt, Rinehart, 1972).

Raffel, Burton, *Ezra Pound: The Prime Minister of Poetry* (Hamden, Conn.: Archon, 1984)

Raffel, Burton, *How to Read a Poem* (N.Y., Meridian, 1984).

Raffel, Burton, *Introduction to Poetry* (N.Y., Signet, 1971).

Raffel, Burton, *T.S. Eliot* (N.Y., Continuum/Ungar, 1982, 1991)

Rees, Joan, ed., *Selected Writings of Fulke Greville* (London, Athlone Press, 1973).

Saintsbury, George, *Historical Manual of English Prosody* (London, Macmillan, 1910).

Schlauch, Margaret, *English Medieval Literature* . . . (London, Oxford U. Press, 1967).

Schipper, Jakob, *A History of English Versification* (Oxord U. Press, 1910).

Scully, James, ed., *Modern Poetics* (N.Y., McGraw-Hill, 1965).

Shapiro, Karl, and Robert Beum, *A Prosody Handbook* (N.Y., Harper, 1965).

Silbajoris, Rimvydas, *Russian Versification* (N.Y., Columbia U. Press, 1968).

Squire, J.C., ed., James Elroy Flecker, *Collected Poems* (N.Y., Knopf, 1928).

Stevick, Robert D., "Introduction," in *One Hundred Middle English Lyrics*, ed. Robert D. Stevick (Indianapolis, Bobbs-Merrill, 1964).

Summers, Joseph H., ed., George Herbert, *Selected Poetry* (N.Y., Signet, 1967).

Turco, Lewis, *The Book of Forms* (N.Y., Dutton, 1968).

Turner, Frederick, *Natural Classicism: Essays on Literature and Science* (N.Y., Paragon, 1985)

Weismiller, Edward, "The 'Dry' and 'Rugged' Verse," in *The Lyric and Dramatic Milton*, ed. Joseph H. Summers (N.Y., Columbia U. Press, 1965).

Wimsatt, W.K., ed., *Versification: Major Language Types*, (N.Y., N.Y.U. Press, 1972).

Woodberry, George Edward, "Introduction," in *The Collected Poems of Rupert Brooke* (N.Y., Dodd, Mead, 1926).

Woods, Susanne, *Natural Emphasis: English Versification from Chaucer to Dryden* (San Marino, Huntington Library, 1984).